dishy desserts

dishy desserts

Vincent Square Books

This edition published in 2004 by Vincent Square
Books, 3 Vincent Square, London SW1P 2LX

First published in 2003

ISBN 1 85626 594 3

Text © see page 176
Photographs © see page 176

The following are hereby identified as the authors of
this work in accordance with Section 77 of the
Copyright, Designs and Patents Act 1988: Darina
Allen, Hugo Arnold, Maddalena Bonino, Ed Baines,
Vatcharin Bhumichitr, Conrad Gallagher, Paul
Gayler, Elisabeth Luard, Alison Price, Oded
Schwartz, Mandy Wagstaff, and Sarah Woodward.

A Cataloguing in Publication record for this title is
available from the British Library.

Printed and bound in China by C & C Offset
Printing Co., Ltd.

contents

introduction

For many people, desserts are the part of the meal we most look forward to. Even the simplest of fresh fruit salads rounds off a meal in a satisfying way, and a really special creation can be the crowning glory of a dinner party.

Desserts all too often fall by the wayside, condemned as being too time-consuming to prepare in our busy lives. And in these health- and weight-conscious days, many people allow themselves a dessert only on special occasions, as a particular treat. But desserts need not be complicated in order to taste good. This book shows that there are desserts for every occasion, from the simplest poached fruit that can be served any night of the week with no more than 10 minutes preparation, to more complex recipes that really push the boat out.

Sometimes it can be harder to choose what to cook than actually to cook it. Follow some simple principles and you can't go wrong. Try to choose seasonal produce - strawberries in June are so much better than the pale imitations available in the shops in the depths of winter. (Although if you have a sudden urge for steamed pudding during a heatwave, don't deny yourself!) Think too about what has gone before in the meal. If you're serving a simple piece of grilled fish or meat for the main course, a luscious slice of tart or chocolate fondant might go down well. If you have served a heavy main course, it might be better to finish with a sorbet, or fresh fruit. Anything involving chocolate always seems to go down well - no matter what has gone before, everyone somehow manages to eat it!

If you are cooking for guests, take some time to plan your menu. If you know you won't have much time to spend in the kitchen on the night, choose a dessert that can be prepared in advance and left in the fridge or freezer until it's needed. If you're planning a casual supper where everyone chips in, you can plan a dessert that can be prepared at the last minute. If you are serving a cheese course, the jury's out as to whether you should serve cheese before dessert or the other way round. British tradition is to offer dessert before cheese but you might prefer to follow the continental example and finish on something sweet instead.

Presentation is important where desserts are concerned. Remember that we all 'eat with our eyes' before the food even gets to our plate and a beautifully presented pudding will be the crowning glory of any meal. Try adding a dusting of icing sugar over a simple fruit compote or placing a sprig of mint in a bowl of luscious red strawberries. A plain cake can be transformed into a magnificent gâteau with the addition of whipped cream and piled fruit. Chocolate curls add sophistication to ice creams and chocolate coffee beans make a statement on a mousse or fondant.

Always try to choose the best-quality produce for your desserts. Choosing the freshest fruit and using chocolate with a high cocoa content will make a real difference to the finished product. Most of the ingredients used in these recipes are easily available in the high street - even produce which would have been considered exotic a few years ago is on sale in the produce section of most supermarkets. Other ingredients might take a little more effort to track down but many can be found in Asian or Caribbean shops or markets.

tips & shortcuts

use your freezer

Many varieties of fruit are now available in frozen form nowadays, and make a good standby for quickly prepared desserts. Top frozen fruit with crumble mixture and bake for a quick family pudding, or make a fruit compote by warming the fruit with red wine, sugar and vanilla seeds. Serve with crème fraîche for a fresh and satisfying dessert.

convenience foods

Pastry is not difficult to make, but if you simply don't have the time, there are various products found in most supermarkets that will make your life easier. Filo, sweet and puff pastry are all available. For a quick pudding, simply roll out squares of puff pastry, top with fresh fruit and a dusting of sugar and bake for a few minutes. Filo pastry can be made into little purse shapes, or laid on top of fruit in a gratin dish to add the satisfying crunch of pastry without the same calorific content.

healthy desserts

All of us should be aiming to eat at least 5 portions of fruit and vegetables per day. A portion counts as a slice of melon, an apple or half a grapefruit, 3 tablespoons of cooked vegetables such as peas, sweetcorn or carrots, or a cereal-bowl of salad. The health-giving benefits of increasing fruit and vegetables consumption are generally recognised. A fruit-based dessert can go to make up part of those five portions a day, so there's really no reason to deprive yourself!

how to use this book

Each recipe provides information about the number of servings it provides, and how long it takes to prepare and cook. As a general principle, the preparation time is the time it takes to wash, prepare and chop the ingredients for the recipe, and the cooking time is the time you actually need to spend cooking, although for much of this time the dish may be able to be left to its own devices while you get on with something else.

In addition, each recipe provides nutritional information. As a rough guide, children, sedentary women and older adults need approximately 1,600 calories per day. Teenage girls, active women and sedentary men need 2,200 calories, and teenage boys, active men and very active women need up to 2,800 per day.

There is information about the amount of fats per serving. Current advice is that no more than 10-30 per cent of our daily energy intake should come from fats. Most of us should be trying to cut down on total fats, particularly saturated fats. Carbohydrates are given next - they are an important part of everyone's diet. It is recommended that at least a third of our daily intake is made up of starchy foods such as potatoes, yams, bread, pasta, noodles, chapattis, rice, sweet potatoes and so on.

It is recommended that our daily salt intake not exceed 6g. Most of us consume more like 9g (the equivalent of 2 teaspoonfuls). Much of the salt we consume comes from processed convenience foods, but approximately 10 per cent of it comes from salt we add to our food, either during cooking or at the table. High salt consumption is implicated in raised blood pressure, which is turn has been linked to a higher risk of heart disease and stroke.

fruit-
based
desserts

mango soufflé with lime sabayon

4-6 mangoes, peeled and diced
50ml (2fl oz) water
juice and zest of 3 limes
5 egg whites
50g (2oz) caster sugar, plus extra for dusting
butter for greasing

Lime sauce
3 limes
3 tablespoons light brown sugar
25g (1oz) unsalted butter
200ml (7fl oz) double cream

Place the mangoes in a pan with the water over gentle heat. Simmer for 5 minutes. Add the lime juice and zest. Purée in a food processor and set aside.

Preheat the oven to 180°C/350°F/gas mark 4.

Beat the egg whites in a large bowl and gently add the caster sugar. With a metal spoon fold the mango purée into the egg mixture. Butter 4 medium-sized soufflé dishes and dust with caster sugar, making sure the dishes are completely coated. Gently pour in the mango mixture and lightly smooth the top. Cook the soufflés for 25 minutes, or until the top has browned and risen.

For the sauce, grate the rind of 2 limes. Mix the zest with the juice of all 3 limes and pour into a small pan. Add the brown sugar and cook over a low heat until the sugar has dissolved. Add the butter and allow to melt, then pour in the cream and stir thoroughly. Bring the sauce to the boil, and let it bubble for 2 minutes until the cream has thickened. Pour the sauce into a jug.

Serve the soufflés immediately they are ready, with the sauce.

Nutritional value per serving:
Calories: 408
Fats: 30g
Carbohydrates: 32g
Salt: 0.27g

nectarines with honey & sauternes

100g (3^1/$_2$oz) caster sugar

1 tablespoon small mint leaves, stalks removed

4 large nectarines

25g (1oz) unsalted butter

75ml (3fl oz) lavender honey

grated zest of ^{1}/$_4$ lemon

^{1}/$_2$ teaspoon lavender pollen (see TIP)

100ml (3^1/$_2$fl oz) Sauternes or other sweet
   dessert wine

4 tablespoons flaked almonds, lightly toasted

Combine the sugar with 500ml (18fl oz) of water in a saucepan and bring slowly to the boil, stirring to dissolve the sugar. Add the stalks from the mint leaves, then the nectarines and simmer for 5 minutes, turning the nectarines occasionally if the liquid doesn't cover them completely. Remove from the heat and set aside. When the nectarines are cool enough to handle, peel them, cut in half and remove the stones. Return the nectarine halves to the cooked syrup (this may all be done well in advance).

To serve, melt the butter in a large frying pan and stir in the honey, lemon zest and lavender pollen. Drain the nectarines, toss them in the honey mixture and then pour in the Sauternes. Turn the nectarines in the pan until glazed all over. Place the nectarines on serving plates, coat with the lavender honey sauce, scatter over the toasted flaked almonds and mint leaves and serve.

TIP

Lavender pollen is the name given to ground lavender flowers. To make, simply dry the flowers, then place in a mortar or blender and blitz to a fine powder. Use to flavour all manner of dishes: for instance add to pasta with chopped parsley and walnuts, or to ricotta with lemon and lime zest and cream to make a wonderful mousse.

Nutritional value per serving:

Calories: 342

Fats: 11g

Carbohydrates: 56g

Salt: 0.03g

spicy papaya & melon salad

juice of 1–2 limes

6 tablespoons sugar

1 hot red chilli

1–2 papayas, peeled, deseeded and diced

1 small ripe melon, deseeded and diced

Put the lime juice and sugar in a small pan with its own volume of water. Bring gently to the boil, stirring to dissolve the sugar crystals. Add the chilli, remove from the heat and leave to infuse and cool. Combine the prepared fruits in a bowl and dress with the sugar syrup. Top with the infused chilli as a warning to the unwary.

Nutritional value per serving:

Calories: 151

Fats: 0g

Carbohydrates: 37g

Salt: 0.04g

stuffed apples with **rhubarb crumble** & lavender

600g (1¼lb) rhubarb, chopped

juice and grated zest of 1 orange

75g (3oz) demerara sugar

1 teaspoon ground cinnamon

4 Russet or Golden Delicious apples

150g (5oz) plain flour

1 teaspoon baking powder

75g (3oz) demerara sugar

1 teaspoon lavender pollen (see page 16)

75g (3oz) blanched almonds, chopped (optional)

75g (3oz) unsalted butter, diced

1 teaspoon lavender flowers, to decorate

Put the rhubarb, orange juice and zest, sugar and cinnamon in a saucepan and bring to the boil. Cover and simmer for 8-10 minutes, then cool slightly.

Cut the tops off the apples, about 2cm (¾in) from the top, and with a small teaspoon carefully scoop out the core and pips. Fill the apples with the rhubarb mixture.

Preheat the oven to 180°C/350°F/gas mark 4. For the topping, sift the flour and baking powder into a bowl and stir in the sugar, lavender pollen and almonds, if using. Rub the butter into the flour mixture until it resembles breadcrumbs. Sprinkle the crumble mixture over the apples, pressing down lightly to form a crust.

Place the apples in a buttered ovenproof dish and bake for 35-40 minutes, until they are tender and the crumble is golden and crisp. Decorate with the lavender flowers and serve with lashings of cream or good old custard.

Nutritional value per serving:

Calories: 598

Fats: 27g

Carbohydrates: 85g

Salt: 0.42g

baked almond-stuffed **peaches**

4 peaches

100g (3½oz) amaretti biscuits, crumbled

1 egg

2 tablespoons roughly chopped blanched whole
  almonds

2 tablespoons light brown sugar

butter, for greasing

Preheat the oven to 180°C/350°F/gas mark 4. Halve the peaches and remove the stones. Combine the amaretti, egg, almonds and sugar. Stuff the peaches with this mixture.

Generously butter an ovenproof dish and arrange the peaches in it, cut sides up. Pour in 150ml (¼ pint) of water and bake, uncovered, in the preheated oven for 30 minutes, or until the peaches are tender but short of collapsing.

Nutritional value per serving:
Calories: 251
Fats: 10g
Carbohydrates: 38g
Salt: 0.36g

mango & passion fruit trifle

8 amaretti biscuits, roughly broken

200g (7oz) panettone

8 tablespoons very sweet thick sherry,
   preferably Pedro Ximenez

2 mangoes, peeled and roughly chopped

4 passion fruit

150ml ($^1/_4$ pint) whipping cream

40g ($1^1/_2$oz) caster sugar

Put half the crushed amaretti into the bottom of 4 glasses. Break the panettone up into bite-sized pieces and divide equally among the 4 glasses. Drizzle a tablespoon of sherry into each one.

Add the chopped mango to the glasses, together with the pulp scooped out of the passion fruit.

Whip the cream with the sugar until standing in soft peaks, fold in the remaining sherry and spoon over the top of the other ingredients.

Top with the remaining amaretti biscuits and serve.

Nutritional value per serving:

Calories: 565

Fats: 24g

Carbohydrates: 77g

Salt: 0.46g

poached plums

200g (7oz) sugar
225ml (8fl oz) cold water
450g (1lb) fresh plums, stoned

Put the sugar and water into a saucepan and bring slowly to the boil. Add the plums; cover and simmer until the plums are soft and bursting. Turn into a bowl and serve chilled with pouring cream.

TIP
Try substituting apricots for the plums.

Nutritional value per serving:
Calories: 235
Fats: 0g
Carbohydrates: 62g
Salt: 0.02g

pears in honey & saffron

4 firm pears
2 heaped tablespoons honey
juice of 1 lemon
225ml (8fl oz) water
1 stick cinnamon
2 cloves
1 teaspoon saffron strands

Peel the pears, leaving the stalks intact. Put the honey and lemon juice in a heavy-bottomed pan into which the pears will fit snugly and place over a moderate heat. Stir until the honey has melted then add the water and spices. Keep stirring until the liquid comes to the boil then turn down the heat and leave to simmer for 5 minutes. Now add the pears to the liquid and simmer for 20 minutes, turning carefully halfway through and basting the pears regularly with the sauce. Leave the pears to cool in the syrup before serving.

Nutritional value per serving:
Calories: 108
Fats: 0g
Carbohydrates: 27g
Salt: 0.03g

pavlova with frozen raspberry yogurt

whites of 6 eggs
350g (12oz) caster sugar
vegetable oil, for brushing

Frozen raspberry yoghurt
2 punnets of raspberries
50g (2oz) caster sugar
2 drops of vanilla essence
1 teaspoon lemon juice
2 egg yolks
500ml (18fl oz) plain runny yogurt

First make the frozen raspberry yogurt: put the raspberries in a large saucepan with the sugar and vanilla essence, 2 tablespoons of water and the lemon juice. Bring to the boil, purée and allow to cool. Fill another pan one-third full of water and bring to the boil, then reduce to simmer. Put the egg yolks and a teaspoon of water in a heatproof bowl and place over the pan. Whisk the egg yolks until pale and fluffy, remove from the heat and continue to whisk for another 30 seconds. Fold two-thirds of the cooled raspberry purée into the egg yolk mix and add the yogurt. Fold together and place in an ice-cream machine for 40-60 minutes.

Make the pavlova: turn your oven on at the lowest possible setting. Bring another pan half-filled with water to the boil and again place a clean bowl over it. After 2 minutes, remove the warmed bowl and pour the egg whites into it. Whisk vigorously, adding the sugar slowly, a tablespoon at a time, into the egg whites. Continue whisking until the egg whites are firm and peaking with a glossy sheen. Place greaseproof paper on 2 oven trays and brush with oil. Put 6 dollops of the meringue mixture on to each tray, leaving at least 7.5cm (3in) between each. Place in the oven for $1^3/_4$-2 hours.

Once the meringues are cooked (when tapped gently they sound hollow), remove from the oven and allow to cool. When they are cool, use a bread knife to cut each meringue in half like a roll. Take curled scoops of your iced yogurt by dragging a dessertspoon over the yogurt's surface, place one in the middle of each meringue base, pop the top back on and press down gently. Once all of the meringues are stuffed, pour the remaining raspberry purée over their tops and serve on a large dish.

Nutritional value per serving:
Calories: 538
Fats: 5g
Carbohydrates: 119g
Salt: 0.5g

strawberry tiramisu

310g (11oz) mascarpone cheese
175g (6oz) boudoir sponge fingers
250ml (9fl oz) sweet dessert wine
   (Sauternes or similar)
310g (11oz) strawberries, hulled
250ml (9fl oz) double cream

Spoon half of the mascarpone on to the bottom of a serving bowl. Pour the wine into a shallow dish and dip in the sponge fingers before arranging them over the mascarpone, breaking them up as necessary.

Cover with half the strawberries and then spread the rest of the mascarpone on the top, smoothing down the top with a palette knife that has been briefly dipped in boiling water. Chill for at least two hours or overnight.

To serve, scatter over the remaining strawberries and bring to the table for maximum effect. Spoon into glass dishes to serve.

Nutritional value per serving:
Calories: 579
Fats: 45g
Carbohydrates: 33g
Salt: 0.27g

strawberry sundae

2 egg whites

pinch of salt

110g (4oz) caster sugar

700g (1½lb) strawberries, cleaned, hulled and
  halved

juice of half a lemon

icing sugar to taste

225ml (8fl oz) whipping cream

To assemble

175ml (6fl oz) whipping cream

8 large strawberries

8 sprigs of mint or borage

Nutritional value per serving:

Calories: 278

Fats: 20g

Carbohydrates: 24g

Salt: 0.23g

Preheat the oven to 130°C/250°F/gas mark ½. Line two baking trays with baking parchment.

Place the egg whites in a large bowl along with the salt. Using an electric beater, whisk into stiff peaks. Add half the caster sugar and continue whisking until thick and glossy, 2–3 minutes. Add the remaining sugar in a steady stream whilst continually beating. Fill the meringue into a piping bag fitted with a medium-sized nozzle. Pipe 5cm (2in) meringues evenly spaced on to the baking parchment. You will have approximately 24 meringues. Bake in the preheated oven for 45 minutes. Turn off the oven and allow the meringues to cool inside. Store in an airtight container until required.

Place the strawberries in a blender or food processor along with the lemon juice. Process until roughly chopped then add the icing sugar. Process for a few seconds more. You will have about 850ml (1½ pints) of purée.

Reserve 300ml (½ pint) of the purée and refrigerate until required. Place the remainder in the bowl of an ice-cream maker with the cream. Churn until frozen. Transfer to a freezeproof container and freeze until required.

Chill eight tall glasses on a tray in the fridge for 15 minutes. Lightly whip the remaining cream to soft peaks. Place a small scoop of ice cream in the base of each glass, add a crushed meringue, top with a spoonful of cream and a drizzle of the reserved strawberry purée. Repeat with two more layers of each. Place a strawberry and a sprig of mint or borage on top of each sundae and serve immediately with long spoons.

two-pepper red wine strawberries

150ml (¼ pint) good-quality red wine, preferably Cabernet Sauvignon

4 tablespoons caster sugar

½ teaspoon black peppercorns, coarsely cracked

5cm (2in) piece of vanilla pod

1 teaspoon cornflour

25g (1oz) unsalted butter

450g (1lb) strawberries

½ teaspoon green peppercorns, drained

vanilla ice cream, to serve

mint leaves, to decorate

Put the wine in a saucepan, holding back 2 tablespoons of it, and add the sugar and half the black pepper. Add the vanilla seeds, and the pod, and stir over a moderate heat to dissolve the sugar. Bring to the boil. Mix the 2 tablespoons of wine with the cornflour and add to the pan. Cook gently for 1-2 minutes, until the mixture has thickened slightly. Remove the sauce from the heat and take out the vanilla pod.

Melt the butter in a frying pan over a high heat, add the strawberries and the remaining black pepper and cook for 1 minute. Pour over the wine sauce and return to the boil. Add the green peppercorns, then pour into a bowl and leave to cool. Refrigerate overnight to allow the flavours to develop. To serve, put the strawberry mixture in cocktail glasses, top with vanilla ice cream and decorate with mint leaves.

How to remove vanilla seeds

To remove the seeds from a vanilla pod, make a slit along the length of the pod with a sharp knife then carefully run the tip of the knife from one end of the slit to the other.

Nutritional value per serving:

Calories: 168

Fats: 5g

Carbohydrates: 24g

Salt: 0.03g

mixed berries with champagne sabayon

300ml ($^1/_2$ pint) Champagne

50g (2oz) caster sugar

4 egg yolks

100g ($3^1/_2$oz) blackberries

100g ($3^1/_2$oz) raspberries

100g ($3^1/_2$oz) redcurrants, stalks removed

Place the Champagne in a pan with the sugar and simmer for a few minutes until the sugar dissolves, stirring occasionally. Remove from the heat and allow to cool a little. Place the egg yolks in a large heatproof bowl set over a pan of simmering water and whisk until well combined and just heated through. Gradually pour in the Champagne mixture, a little at a time until completely combined, whisking continuously.

Continue to whisk the sabayon until the mixture has doubled in size, being careful not to allow the mixture to become too hot or the sabayon may split – this should take no more than 6–8 minutes. Remove the bowl from the heat and allow to cool.

To serve, preheat the grill until it is very hot. Arrange the berries in a wide-rimmed dish and spoon over enough of the sabayon to just cover. Place under the grill for a few minutes until golden. Serve immediately.

TIP

Sabayon is a classic French sauce and once you get the hang of it, it's a doddle to make. It will keep happily for a couple of hours, covered with cling film in the fridge, but after that it starts to lose some of its volume.

Nutritional value per serving:

Calories: 184

Fats: 6g

Carbohydrates: 20g

Salt: 0.04g

warm **berries** on toasted panettone with clotted cream

75g (3oz) redcurrant jelly

juice of 1 lemon

1–2 tablespoons brandy

4 slices of panettone

75g (3oz) strawberries

75g (3oz) blueberries

75g (3oz) blackberries

75g (3oz) raspberries

icing sugar for dusting

clotted cream, to serve

Gently melt the redcurrant jelly with the lemon juice and brandy in a frying pan. Meanwhile, toast the panettone slices on both sides and keep warm.

When the jelly has melted and is well blended with the other ingredients, add all the berries and toss gently, coating the fruit.

Place the toasted panettone on serving plates, spoon on the hot fruit and dust with icing sugar. Serve with a dollop of clotted cream.

Nutritional value per serving:

Calories: 391

Fats: 13g

Carbohydrates: 64g

Salt: 0.42g

champagne berry jelly

unscented vegetable oil, for greasing

250g (9oz) fraises de bois

250g (9oz) redcurrants

250g (9oz) whitecurrants

250g (9oz) golden raspberries

250g (9oz) blueberries

250g (9oz) loganberies

10 leaves of gelatine

150g (5oz) caster sugar

150ml ($^{1}/_{4}$ pint) water

1 bottle (750ml/1$^{1}/_{4}$ pints) pink Champagne

Brush 10 tall jelly moulds (holding about 150ml/$^{1}/_{4}$ pint) with a little unscented vegetable oil. Pick over the fruit, wash and dry well. Soak gelatine as shown below. In a pan, bring the sugar and water to the boil. Reduce the heat and simmer for about 5 minutes to form a clear syrup. Remove from the heat. Squeeze out excess water from the gelatine then dissolve it in the syrup. Add the Champagne, stir and strain through a fine sieve into a large jug. Place the jelly moulds onto a tray that will fit inside your fridge. Pour in enough jelly to coat the base of the moulds – about 7mm ($^{1}/_{4}$in). Leave to set in the fridge. When set, remove from the fridge and half-fill the moulds with fruit. Pour in enough jelly to cover three quarters of the fruit (any more and the fruit will float). Leave to set in the refrigerator then fill to the top with the remaining jelly to encase the fruit entirely. Leave to set in the fridge. Serve with pistachio ice cream or biscuits.

How to soak gelatine leaves

Gelatine comes in small stiff transparent sheets - soak them in cold water until they become soft, then squeeze out the excess water and continue with recipe.

Nutritional value per serving:

Calories: 185

Fats: 2g

Carbohydrates: 27g

Salt: 0.08g

SERVES 4-6

PREPARATION TIME: 5 MINUTES

COOKING TIME: 35 MINUTES

FREEZING TIME: 1 HOUR

blackcurrant leaf sorbet

275g (10oz) caster sugar
600ml (1 pint) water
zest and juice of 1 lemon
3 handfuls of blackcurrant leaves

Combine the sugar and water in a large pan. Add the lemon zest and stir over a gentle heat until the sugar has dissolved. Turn up the heat and allow the syrup to boil for 5 minutes. Remove from the heat and add the blackcurrant leaves and lemon juice. Cover with a lid and leave to infuse for 30 minutes. Strain through a sieve lined with a square of damp muslin. Pour into the bowl of an ice-cream machine and churn until frozen. Transfer to a freezerproof container and freeze until required.

Serve in small scoops in well-chilled glasses.

TIP

Select young blackcurrant leaves as these give a fresh taste, and do not allow them to infuse for longer than half an hour as the resulting syrup may be sour and inedible.

Nutritional value per serving:
Calories: 273
Fats: 0g
Carbohydrates: 73g
Salt: 0.01g

gooseberry & elderflower charlotte

1 sachet gelatine (10g/^{1}/$_2$oz)

2 tablespoons water

450g (1lb) gooseberries, topped and tailed

75g (3oz) caster sugar

2 tablespoons elderflower cordial

2 tablespoons water

1 strip lemon zest

125g (4^1/$_2$oz) sponge fingers

1 dessertspoon elderflower cordial diluted with
   2 tablespoons water

300ml (10fl oz) double cream

300ml (10fl oz) fromage frais

110g (4oz) caster sugar

25ml (1fl oz) water

2 egg whites

150ml (5fl oz) whipped cream

elderflower heads, to decorate

Nutritional value per serving:

Calories: 588

Fats: 36g

Carbohydrates: 60g

Salt: 0.23g

Sprinkle the gelatine over the water in a small ramekin. Place the gooseberries in a large pan with the sugar, elderflower cordial, water and lemon zest. Cover and cook very gently for 5-6 minutes until soft. Don't worry if the fruits break up slightly. Add the soaked gelatine and stir to dissolve. Cool slightly, then press through a nylon sieve. Set aside and do not allow to set.

Brush the unsugared side of the sponge fingers with a little of the diluted elderflower cordial and use to line the sides of a 1.2 litre (2 pint) charlotte tin. Whip the cream to soft peaks and fold in the fromage frais. Fold into the cooled gooseberry purée.

Place the sugar and water in a heavy-based pan. Cook over a low heat until the sugar dissolves. Wash down the sides of the pan with a clean brush dipped in cold water. Bring to the boil and insert a sugar thermometer. After 1 minute place the egg whites in a large bowl and whisk to stiff peaks. When the syrup reaches the soft ball stage on the sugar thermometer 116°C (240°F), remove from the heat and pour in a thin, steady stream on to the egg whites while continually whisking. Continue whisking until the meringue is cold, thick and glossy.

Stir a couple of spoonfuls of the meringue into the gooseberry mixture to loosen it. Then fold in the remainder. Carefully spoon the mousse into the prepared charlotte tin. Refrigerate for several hours or overnight. To turn out, turn the point of a knife round the top edge of the charlotte. Dip the mould briefly into a basin of hot water, invert on to a serving plate and the dessert will slide out. Decorate with whipped cream and elderflower heads.

hedgerow trifle

3 large macaroons

4 tablespoons sherry or brandy

4 tablespoons blueberry or blackberry jam

350g (12oz) fruits from the hedgerow such as
    bilberries, blackberries or wild raspberries,
    washed and dried

250g (9oz) marscapone

50g (2oz) caster sugar

1-2 tablespoons milk

400ml (14fl oz) milk

1 vanilla pod, split

1 whole egg

3 egg yolks

40g (1¹/₂oz) caster sugar

40g (1¹/₂oz) plain flour

125ml (4fl oz) whipping cream

a few extra berries, to decorate

Cut each macaroon into 6 pieces and lay in a large glass serving bowl, or divide between 4 tall glasses. Spoon over the sherry or brandy. Warm the jam and spread over the macaroons. Pile the washed and dried fruits on top.

Combine the marscapone with the sugar and enough milk to give a soft consistency. Spread evenly over the fruits. Chill in the refrigerator.

Combine the milk and split vanilla pod in a saucepan and bring to the boil. Whisk the whole egg, egg yolks and sugar until thick and pale. Stir in the flour. Pour a little of the boiling milk onto the eggs, stir to blend, then return to the pan with the remainder of the milk. Cook, stirring, until the custard thickens and boiling point is reached. The flour will prevent the custard from curdling. Cook for 2 more minutes. Transfer to a clean bowl, dab the top with a little extra milk to prevent a skin forming, then set aside to cool. Whisk the custard to ensure it is smooth before spooning over the trifle.

Decorate with whipped cream and a few extra berries.

Nutritional value per serving:
Calories: 527
Fats: 34g
Carbohydrates: 47g
Salt: 0.3g

cherry clafoutis

Cherry compote
50g (2oz) caster sugar
900g (2lb) fresh cherries, pitted
3 tablespoons kirsch

Clafoutis batter
50g (2oz) butter, melted
50g (2oz) caster sugar to coat moulds
6 large eggs
310g (11oz) caster sugar
175g (6oz) plain flour, sifted
300ml ($^1/_2$ pint) crème fraîche or double cream
300ml ($^1/_2$ pint) full-fat milk
2 tablespoons kirsch
icing sugar, to dust

In a pan gently heat the sugar in 1 tablespoon of water until dissolved. Add the cherries and kirsch, and cook on a low heat for 15 minutes, or until the cherries are soft but still whole. Remove from the heat. Drain half the cherries, leaving the rest in the liquid.

Preheat the oven to 180°C/350°F/gas mark 4. Grease the inside of a large baking dish with melted butter and caster sugar, then put aside. In a mixer, whisk the eggs until frothy, add sugar; then whisk for a further 2 minutes. Add the flour, crème fraîche or cream, milk and kirsch, then whisk until well blended. Place the drained, cooked cherries in the baking dish, pour over the batter and place on a baking sheet. Bake for 15 minutes then remove the clafoutis from the oven and top up with any remaining batter. Return to the oven for 15 minutes until the clafoutis is golden in colour and firm to touch.

Remove, dust with icing sugar and place on plates with a spoonful of compote. Serve.

TIP
A sweet white dessert wine such as Muscat Beaume de Venise goes perfectly with this traditional French baked pudding.

Nutritional value per serving:
Calories: 489
Fats: 20g
Carbohydrates: 70g
Salt: 0.37g

apple pecorino strudel

50g (2oz) fresh white breadcrumbs

50g (2oz) ground almonds

110g (4oz) unsalted butter

900g (2lb) cooking apples, peeled, cored and
   thinly sliced

50g (2oz) caster sugar

1 teaspoon ground cinnamon

$1/2$ teaspoon ground mixed spice

50g (2oz) raisins, soaked in water until plump

25g (1oz) walnuts or almonds, chopped

zest of half a lemon

150g (5oz) Pecorino Romano, thinly sliced

4 large sheets of filo pastry, about 45 x 30cm
   (18 x 12in)

icing sugar, for dusting

Preheat the oven to 200°C/400°F/gas mark 6. Fry the breadcrumbs and ground almonds in half of the butter until lightly golden, then set aside.

Mix together the apples, sugar, cinnamon, mixed spice, raisins, nuts and lemon zest. Carefully fold in the Pecorino cheese.

Melt the remaining butter. Lay out 1 sheet of filo dough on a work surface and brush with some of the butter, then top with the remaining sheets of filo, brushing with butter between the layers. Brush the final sheet of pastry with more butter and sprinkle the fried breadcrumb mixture over the top. Spread the apple mixture over the surface and roll up the pastry to form a compact roll. Transfer to a greased baking sheet, curving the strudel to fit if necessary, and brush with the remaining melted butter. Bake for 20-25 minutes, until crisp and golden.

Remove from the oven, dust generously with icing sugar and serve hot.

TIP

Ricotta makes a tasty alternative to the Pecorino.

Nutritional value per serving:

Calories: 533

Fats: 31g

Carbohydrates: 51g

Salt: 1.34g

passion fruit pyramid

Meringue
12 egg whites
500g (1lb 2oz) caster sugar

Passion fruit cream
30 whole passion fruit, halved, juices and pips
   scooped out, sieved to yield 200ml (7fl oz)
   purée
250ml (9fl oz) water
800ml (1½ pints) double cream
250g (9oz) sugar
75g (3oz) cornflour
10 egg yolks
175g (6oz) unsalted butter, cut into cubes
3 passion fruit
8 mangos, peeled and sliced

Garnish
icing sugar
6 passion fruit
edible flowers, such as violets, fresh or
   crystallised

Nutritional value per serving:
Calories: 515
Fats: 29g
Carbohydrates: 62g
Salt: 0.17g

Preheat the oven to 110°C/225°F/gas mark ¼. Taking four sheets of silicone paper, draw a 30.5cm (12in) circle on the first, on the second a 25.5cm (10in) circle, on the third a 20cm (8in) circle and on the fourth a 15cm (6in) circle. Place these sheets on baking trays. Whisk the egg whites with 100g (3½oz) of the sugar until it forms stiff peaks. Continue to whisk, adding the sugar gradually. Once all the sugar is added, the egg whites should be stiff and glossy. Fill a piping bag with this mixture and pipe to fill each of the paper circles. Bake for 8-10 hours until the meringue is dry and hard to the touch, leave to cool, then layer with non-stick paper and store in airtight containers.

In a heavy-based pan, bring the passion fruit purée, the water, 50ml (2fl oz) cream and the sugar to the boil, stirring continuously. Mix the cornflour with a little cold water then add to the boiling mixture, stirring. Reduce the heat and cook for 5 minutes, stirring to prevent it from burning. Remove from heat and leave to cool for about 2 minutes. Beat in the egg yolks then the butter. Cover with non-stick paper and leave to cool. Cut the 3 passion fruit in half, squeeze out the juice and pips and add these to the mixture. Whisk the remaining cream until it holds its shape and fold into the passion fruit.

Pipe a blob of cream in the centre of a glass cake stand to prevent the meringue from sliding around. Place the largest disc of meringue on the stand and spread with cream, leaving a 2.5cm (1in) rim of meringue. Top with a layer of mango, then the next meringue disc. Repeat the process twice to finish with the smallest disc of meringue. Dust with icing sugar and arrange remaining slices of fresh or oven-dried mango on the top, squeezing over the juice of the 6 passion fruits. Decorate the sides with fresh or crystallised flowers.

lemon meringue pie

50g (2oz) butter, plus more for greasing

1 pack of sweet shortcrust pastry

juice of 6 lemons and grated zest of 4

1 tablespoon apricot jam

9 egg yolks

175g (6oz) caster sugar

200ml (7fl oz) double cream

300g (10½oz) icing sugar

Meringue

350g (12oz) caster sugar

whites of 6 eggs

TIP

If you like, you can make a lemon sauce for the pie by sieving 3-4 tablespoons of lemon marmalade into a small pan, adding an equal amount of water and heating gently, stirring until syrupy.

Nutritional value per serving:

Calories: 698

Fats: 32g

Carbohydrates: 124g

Salt: 0.74g

Preheat the oven to 180°C/350°F/gas mark 4 and butter a 25cm (10in) tart pan. Roll out the pastry to fit the pan, sprinkling with the grated zest of 1 lemon as you roll. Line the tart pan with the pastry and cover with a piece of greaseproof paper. Cover that with baking beans or dry rice and bake blind for 15-20 minutes until lightly coloured. Remove from the oven and allow to cool, turning the oven setting down to 150°C/300°F/gas mark 2.

While the tart shell is cooling, in a small saucepan mix the apricot jam with 1 tablespoon of water and heat gently until you have a syrup (take care not to let it burn). Remove the beans or rice and paper from the tart shell and brush the pastry with the apricot syrup. Leave this to set while you make the filling.

Mix the egg yolks and caster sugar together in a saucepan and bring to a gentle heat, then add the cream, lemon juice and remaining zest, together with butter, stirring continuously so the mixture does not curdle. Pour the lemon mix into the cooled tart shell and place in the oven for 10 minutes. Once the tart is cooked, remove it from the oven and allow to cool.

While it cools, make the meringue: using a spotlessly clean bowl and whisk, put 1 tablespoon of the sugar in the bottom of the bowl, add the egg whites and beat vigorously until they are standing in soft peaks. Slowly add the remaining sugar, beating constantly, until the egg whites are standing in firm peaks.

Dust the cooled tart with icing sugar, spoon over meringue mixture and place under the grill for about 1 or 2 minutes, until the meringue browns slightly.

blueberry pancakes with crème fraîche

110g (4oz) plain flour

1 tablespoon caster sugar

2 tablespoons double cream

2 eggs, separated

grated zest of 1 lemon

225ml (8fl oz) milk

unsalted butter

110g (4oz) blueberries

4-6 tablespoons maple syrup

4 tablespoons crème fraîche

Sift the flour into a bowl, mix in the sugar and make a well in the centre. In a separate bowl mix the cream, egg yolks, lemon zest and milk. Pour into the well in the flour and mix thoroughly, using a small whisk or wooden spoon to make a smooth batter.

Whisk the egg whites until stiff. Gently spoon a third into the batter to loosen the texture, then fold in the rest.

Melt a small knob of butter in a 15cm (6in) frying pan. Pour in a quarter of the batter; the pancakes should not be more than 1cm ($^1/_2$in) thick. Sprinkle some blueberries on the surface. When small bubbles begin to break on the surface, flip the pancake over and and cook for another minute or two. Slide onto a warm plate, drizzle with maple syrup and keep warm.

Make 3 more pancakes. Serve each helping with a dollop of crème fraîche.

TIP

The secret of light pancakes is to leave the batter in the fridge for 30 minutes to rest before cooking.

Nutritional value per serving:

Calories: 330

Fats: 16g

Carbohydrates: 39g

Salt: 0.23g

banana fritters

110g (4oz) plain flour

225ml (8fl oz) coconut milk

$^1/_2$ teaspoon salt

50g (2oz) granulated sugar

1 tablespoon white sesame seeds

6 small or 3 large unripe bananas (the skins just
   turning yellow)

vegetable oil for deep-frying

Combine the flour, coconut milk, salt, sugar and sesame seeds in a bowl and mix to form a smooth batter. Set aside.

If using small bananas, cut in half; if using large bananas, cut into 3 pieces. (You should end up with pieces about 7.5cm (3in) long.) Cut each piece in half lengthways to give strips about 1cm ($^1/_2$in) thick.

Heat the oil in a deep-fryer to 200°C (400°F). Dip the banana strips in the batter, shake off any excess and lower into the hot oil. Fry until golden brown, then remove, drain on kitchen paper and serve immediately.

Nutritional value per serving:

Calories: 568

Fats: 31g

Carbohydrates: 71g

Salt: 0.79g

swiss chard & pear tart

110g (4oz) raisins or sultanas

2 tablespoons dark rum

900g (2lb) Swiss chard, stalks removed, leaves
   cooked and finely chopped

50g (2oz) pine kernels

75g (3oz) icing sugar, plus extra for dusting

3 pears, peeled, cored and diced

3 tablespoons cream cheese

grated zest of 1 lemon

2 free-range eggs, beaten

Pastry

350g (12oz) plain flour

225g (8oz) unsalted butter, diced
   (at room temperature)

pinch of salt

110g (4oz) icing sugar, sifted

finely grated zest of ½ lemon

1 free-range egg, beaten

Nutritional value per serving:

Calories: 829

Fats: 44g

Carbohydrates: 100g

Salt: 0.76 g

For the pastry, sift the flour on to a work surface and make a well in the centre. Put the butter, salt, sugar and lemon zest in the well and then add the egg. With your fingertips, gradually bring the flour into the centre, blending in the butter, until all the ingredients come together into a soft dough. Knead very lightly for 1 minute, until completely smooth, then form the dough into a ball. Wrap in cling film and leave to rest in the refrigerator for 30 minutes.

Preheat the oven to 200°C/400°F/gas mark 6. Roll out the pastry and use to line a 23cm (9in) flan tin, reserving excess pastry for the top. Prick the base with a fork and chill while you prepare the filling.

Soak the raisins or sultanas in the rum for 15 minutes, then place in a saucepan and heat gently until all the liquid has been absorbed. Place the Swiss chard leaves in a bowl with the raisins and all the remaining ingredients. Mix well, then spread the filling in the pastry case and cover the top with the remaining pastry. Seal the edges and make a few vents in the top.

Bake for 45 minutes, until golden brown, then leave to cool. Turn out of the tin, dust with icing sugar and serve.

TIP

If you do not have time to make pastry, you can now buy some good-quality pre-baked pastry cases. Or use the same filling but top with buttered filo pastry.

fennel & caramelised banana stacks

50g (2oz) unsalted butter, melted

8 sheets of filo pastry

4 tablespoons icing sugar, plus extra for dusting

Fennel mousse

1 large fennel bulb, chopped

60g (2½oz) caster sugar

4 free range egg yolks

2 tablespoons custard powder

¼ vanilla pod

4 tablespoons Marie Brizard (or other anise liquor such as Pernod)

2 tablespoons double cream, semi-whipped

Caramelised bananas

110g (4oz) caster sugar

3 large bananas, peeled and cut into slices 2cm (¾in) thick

90ml (3fl oz) Marie Brizard (or other anise liqueur such as Pernod)

Nutritional value per serving:

Calories: 879

Fats: 22g

Carbohydrates: 149g

Salt: 1.13g

First prepare the filo stacks. Preheat the oven to 180°C/350°F/gas mark 4. Brush a baking sheet with melted butter. Place a sheet of filo on a work surface, brush with melted butter, then place another sheet on top. Brush with butter and sprinkle with a tablespoon of icing sugar. Top with another sheet of filo and brush with butter. Add the fourth sheet, brush with butter and sprinkle with more icing sugar. Repeat with remaining four sheets so you have two separate piles. Cut out six 7.5cm (3in) circles from each stack, place on the baking sheet and bake for 5-7 minutes until golden brown. Remove from oven and cool.

For the fennel mousse, put the fennel in a pan, add 40g (1½oz) of the sugar and enough water to cover. Bring to the boil, reduce the heat and simmer for 20-25 minutes until tender. Blitz in a blender to make 120ml (4½fl oz) purée. Put the egg yolks, the remaining sugar and the custard powder in a bowl and whisk until smooth. Scrape out the vanilla seeds. Heat the fennel purée, Marie Brizard and vanilla seeds in a pan and then carefully pour on to the egg mixture, whisking as you do so. Return to the pan and cook for 3-4 minutes, stirring constantly, until thickened. Transfer to a large bowl and leave to cool, then whisk until smooth. Fold in the whipped cream.

For the caramelised bananas, heat the sugar in a heavy-based frying pan over a high heat until it dissolves and forms a caramel. Add the bananas and cook for 1 minute. Pour in the Marie Brizard to form a light anise caramel. Leave to cool. To assemble, place a filo circle in the centre of each serving plate, place a heaped spoonful of fennel mousse in the centre and top with some caramelised banana. Put another filo circle on top and repeat the layers of fennel mousse and banana. Top with a third filo circle. Dust with a little icing sugar, pour around some of the caramel and serve immediately.

exotic
delights

prickly pear with mango

4 prickly pears with their spikes rubbed off

1 orange, juice and zest

3 tablespoons fresh lime juice

1 tablespoon tequila (optional)

3 tablespoons runny honey

1 large mango or 2 smaller ones, diced

Place the orange juice and zest, lime juice, tequila and honey in a small saucepan, bring to the boil and simmer for 10 minutes. Carefully remove the skin of the prickly pears – avoiding any little bumps which might conceal left-behind spines – and mash the flesh together with the juice mixture. Serve spooned over the diced mango.

Nutritional value per serving:

Calories: 118

Fats: 0g

Carbohydrates: 29g

Salt: 0.02g

pumpkin & pecan crème

450g (1lb) fresh pumpkin, seeds removed,
 sliced, skin left on
50g (2oz) unsalted butter
150g (5oz) pecan nuts, plus extra for decoration
6 egg yolks
75g (3oz) caster sugar
500ml (18fl oz) double cream

Preheat the oven to 190°C/375°F/gas mark 5. Smear half of the butter over the pumpkin flesh and roast for about 1 hour or until tender. Leave to cool, then scoop out the flesh and pass it through a fine sieve or vegetable mouli to give 150g (5oz). Reduce the oven to 150°C/300°F/gas mark 2. Toast the pecans in the oven for about 5 minutes, then remove and allow to cool. Place the egg yolks and sugar in a large bowl and whisk until light and fluffy. Place the cream in a pan and bring to the boil, then slowly whisk into the egg mixture. Finally fold in the pumpkin purée. Grease four 200ml (7fl oz) ramekins with the remaining butter, then pour in the pumpkin mixture and top with the pecan halves. Place in a bain-marie and cover with foil. Bake for 40-45 minutes until each ramekin is slightly raised around the edges and just set. Remove the bain-marie from the oven and leave to cool completely, then cover each ramekin with cling film and chill for at least 2 hours or overnight. Decorate with leftover nuts and serve.

How to purée vegetables

A vegetable mouli is a useful piece of kitchen equipment, allowing cooked vegetables, such as pumpkin or potatoes, to be puréed without turning them into a gluey mass.

Nutritional value per serving:
Calories: 1091
Fats: 105g
Carbohydrates: 27g
Salt: 0.16g

SERVES 4-6

PREPARATION TIME: 1 HOUR

COOKING TIME: 15 MINUTES

gold threads

10 jasmine flowers

400ml (14fl oz) water

10 eggs

1 tablespoon vegetable oil

900g (2lb) granulated sugar

Sprinkle the jasmine flowers over the water and leave to infuse for 1 hour. Separate the egg yolks and reserve the whites. Whisk the yolks in a large bowl until thick and creamy, add the egg whites and oil and whisk to combine. Remove the jasmine flowers from the perfumed water and discard. Pour the water into a large saucepan and add the sugar. Heat gently, stirring to dissolve the sugar, then boil rapidly to form a thin syrup. To make the threads, fill your homemade strainer with the egg mixture and drizzle it in thin streams into the simmering sugar syrup, moving it in a circular motion to form nests of threads. Cook for 1 minute or until golden brown, then remove with a skewer and place on a metal tray to cool.

TIP

This Thai dish is often served at birthday parties or prepared as an offering to the monks on special anniversary days.

How to make a homemade strainer

To make a home-made strainer, clean an empty tin can thoroughly. Pierce six holes in the bottom with a hammer and nail and then fill with batter to make the threads.

Nutritional value per serving:

Calories: 1096

Fats: 16g

Carbohydrates: 236g

Salt: 0.47g

pomegranates served with cream

2 large pomegranates, prepared as below

450g (1lb) crème fraîche or Greek yogurt, well
chilled

50g (2oz) granulated sugar

1 tablespoon orange blossom water or a few
drops of vanilla extract

grated zest of $\frac{1}{2}$ lemon

25g (1oz) flaked almonds

4 sprigs mint

Peel the pomegranates as shown below.

Combine the crème fraîche or yogurt with the sugar, orange blossom water and the
lemon zest, and mix well.

In each of 4 tall glasses arrange the pomegranate seed and cream mixture in alternate
layers, finishing with cream. Sprinkle with almonds, decorate with a sprig of mint and serve.

How to peel a pomegranate

Remove the top and base. Then, with a sharp knife, score through the outer peel so
dividing the fruit into segments. With your hands prise the peel from the delicate seeds,
being careful to remove all traces of the thin yellow skin, which is very bitter.

Nutritional value per serving:

Calories: 514

Fats: 42g

Carbohydrates: 28g

Salt: 0.33g

lemongrass, coconut & vanilla pannacotta

1 vanilla pod
2 lemongrass stalks, outer layers removed
350ml (12fl oz) double cream
150ml ($^1/_4$ pint) unsweetened coconut milk
40g (1$^1/_2$oz) caster sugar
1$^1/_2$ gelatine leaves
assortment of exotic fruits (such as mango, papaya, lychee and dragonfruit), peeled and diced, to serve

Passion-fruit-chilli syrup
2 passion fruit, halved
100ml (3$^1/_2$fl oz) stock syrup (see TIP)
juice and grated zest of $^1/_2$ a lime
$^1/_8$ teaspoon deseeded and finely diced red chilli

Cut the vanilla pod in half lengthways and scrape out the seeds with the tip of a sharp knife. Bruise the lemongrass and shred it finely. Heat the cream, coconut milk, vanilla seeds, lemongrass and sugar in a pan but do not let it boil. Meanwhile, cover the gelatine leaves with cold water for 5 minutes, then squeeze out excess water. Remove the cream mixture from the heat, add the softened gelatine and stir until dissolved. Leave to cool, stirring occasionally, then strain into individual tumbler-style glasses and place in the fridge overnight.

For the passion fruit–chilli syrup, scrape the juice and seeds from the passion fruit into a small pan, add the stock syrup and heat gently. Leave for 10-15 minutes to infuse, then strain. Add the lime juice and zest and the diced chilli and leave to cool.

Arrange the exotic fruits on top of the pannacotta, pour over a little of the chilli syrup and serve.

TIP

To make stock syrup, put 225g (8oz) caster sugar in a saucepan with 300ml ($^1/_2$ pint) of water and bring slowly to the boil, stirring until the sugar has dissolved. Boil rapidly for 2 minutes to form a light syrup. Leave to cool, then store in a cool place. Use for sweet sauces, ice creams, sorbets etc.

Nutritional value per serving:
Calories: 580
Fats: 48g
Carbohydrates: 35g
Salt: 0.43g

iced coconut parfait with papaya & lime

9 egg yolks

150g (5oz) caster sugar

9 tablespoons coconut powder

225ml (8fl oz) double cream

225ml (8fl oz) Greek yogurt

2 papaya

zest and juice of 2 limes

Line a 1.2 litre (2 pint) terrine tin with cling film and place it in the freezer. Mix the egg yolks and sugar in a large bowl and cook as shown below. Whisk in the coconut powder. Continue whisking for 10-15 minutes until thick and doubled in volume. Remove the bowl from the heat and continue whisking until the mixture is cold. Whip the cream to the same consistency as the yogurt and lightly fold into the egg mixture with the yogurt. Pour into the prepared tin and freeze for several hours or overnight until firm.

Peel the papaya, cut in half and remove the seeds. Cut the flesh into even slices, grate over the lime zest and squeeze over the juice. Leave to macerate for 30 minutes. Turn out the parfait, remove the cling film and serve in slices accompanied by the fruit.

How to cook using a double boiler

Half fill a saucepan with water and bring to simmering point. Use a Pyrex bowl which fits snugly into the saucepan just above the level of the water.

Nutritional value per serving:

Calories: 397

Fats: 29g

Carbohydrates: 28g

Salt: 0.12g

preserved clementines

250g (9oz) caster sugar

6 star anise

8 cloves

2 cinnamon sticks, broken into 5cm (2in) lengths

6 tablespoons gin

2kg (4lb) clementines, peeled

In a saucepan, combine the caster sugar and spices with 700ml (1¼ pints) of water, cover and bring to the boil. Stir to ensure all the sugar is dissolved, stir in the gin and then set aside to cool.

Pack the clementines loosely into two 1-litre (1¾ pint) sterilised Kilner jars, distributing the spices as evenly as possible, then pour over the syrup. Leave about 1cm (½in) of space at the top of each jar and seal.

Place the jars in a large saucepan and fill with cold water to come almost, but not quite, to the full height of the jars, leaving about 2cm (¾in). Cover and slowly bring to the boil. Reduce the heat and simmer for about 25 minutes. Remove from the pan and allow to cool.

Store the preserved clementines for up to 5 months.

TIP

Serve on their own, or with cream or ice cream.

Nutritional value per serving:

Calories: 219

Fats: 0g

Carbohydrates: 49g

Salt: 0.02g

SERVES 4

PREPARATION TIME: 5 MINUTES

COOKING TIME: 20 MINUTES

FREEZING TIME: 1-3 HOURS

pistachio and rosewater
ice cream

100g (3¹/₂oz) caster sugar

4 egg yolks

37ml (13fl oz) full-cream milk

200ml (7fl oz) whipping cream

pinch of saffron threads, soaked in a
    spoonful or two of water

2 tablespoons coarsely chopped pistachios

2 dessertspoons rosewater

In a large heatproof mixing bowl, combine the sugar and egg yolks, and whisk until pale. Bring the milk up to boiling point in a saucepan, remove from the heat and pour on to the egg and sugar mixture, whisking all the time. Pour into a clean saucepan, place over a moderate heat and stir, making sure the mixture doesn't catch (particularly at the edges) until thick. As soon as a line drawn with your finger through the custard on the back of a spoon remains, remove from the heat and pour into a clean bowl. Combine the custard with the cream and stir in the saffron and the soaking liquid, with the pistachios and rosewater. Transfer to an ice-cream maker and churn until frozen. Remove from the freezer 10–15 minutes before serving.

How to check the custard mixture

If a line drawn with your finger through the mixture on the back of a spoon remains, it is ready. If it overcooks you will end up with sweet scrambled eggs. If you are nervous, pour the mixture through a sieve, which will help to catch the overcooked lumps.

Nutritional value per serving:

Calories: 441

Fats: 32g

Carbohydrates: 33g

Salt: 0.21g

SERVES 10-12

PREPARATION TIME: 20 MINUTES

COOKING TIME: 30 MINUTES

the snake

110g (4oz) whole almonds

310g (11oz) ground almonds

50g (2oz) icing sugar

110g (4oz) caster sugar

125g (4¹/₂oz) unsalted butter, softened

1 teaspoon ground cinnamon

2 teaspoons orange flower water (you could
     also use rosewater)

filo pastry

1 egg yolk

Fry the whole almonds in a knob of the butter until golden brown on both sides – take care they do not burn. Either process them or pound them in a pestle and mortar until you have a slightly crunchy texture. Mix into the ground almonds and add the two sugars, 110g (4oz) of the butter, the cinnamon and orange flower water. With your hands form to a smooth paste and chill for 30 minutes. Preheat the oven to 180°C/350°F/gas mark 4.

Take two sheets of filo pastry and glue them together end to end with a little of the egg yolk. Roll out the almond paste to a tube the thickness of your thumb and lay it the length of the filo pastry. Roll the pastry up so that you have a long tube. Repeat this process until all the almond paste is used.

Fashion one of the tubes of filled pastry into a coil, starting from the centre. Use egg yolk to stick the ends of pastry together and repeat with the remaining rolls until you have a large coil or 'snake'. Place on a buttered baking tray. Melt the remaining butter and brush this over the surface of the pastry. Bake in the preheated oven for 25–30 minutes, until lightly browned. Leave to cool before serving.

How to make the snake

The snake is constructed by making several small rolls and joining them together in a spriral shape.

Nutritional value per serving:

Calories: 429

Fats: 33g

Carbohydrates: 24g

Salt: 0.16g

pineapple bugles

4 baby pineapples

1 x 110g (4oz) packet desiccated coconut

175g (6oz) sugar

2 vanilla pods

2.5cm (1in) piece of fresh ginger,
   finely chopped

1 red chilli, deseeded and finely chopped

juice of 2 limes

4 tablespoons rum

Peel the skins off the pineapples as shown below, leaving the leaves at the top. Pour out the coconut on to a large plate or tray and place to one side.

In a saucepan, mix the sugar, seeds from the vanilla pods, ginger, chilli and the lime juice. Bring to the boil and allow to simmer until the sugar is golden in colour.

Dry the pineapples with a clean kitchen towel. Pour the hot sugar syrup into a tray and roll the pineapples one by one first in the sugar syrup and then in the coconut. Allow to set. To serve, place on a plate covered with flaked ice, pour over the rum and ignite.

TIP

To judge whether or not a pineapple is ripe, tug at one of the inner leaves – it will come away easily if the pineapple is in the right condition.

How to peel a pineapple

Stand the pineapple upright and cut off the skin in slices. With a sharp knife, cut out the 'eyes' by following the diagonal lines they form round the pineapple.

Nutritional value per serving:

Calories: 409

Fats: 16g

Carbohydrates: 60g

Salt: 0.03g

panna 'ri-cotta'

4 tablespoons milk

150ml (¼ pint) double cream

75g (3oz) caster sugar

zest of half an orange

100ml (3½fl oz) freshly made strong
  coffee, preferably espresso

half a vanilla pod, split

2 gelatine leaves

2 tablespoons rum

200g (7oz) firm ricotta, sieved

sprigs of fresh mint, to decorate (optional)

Apricot compote

75g (3oz) caster sugar

75ml (3fl oz) water

juice of half a lemon

350g (12oz) fresh apricots, stoned & sliced

Put the milk, cream, sugar and orange zest in a pan and bring to the boil. Stir in the coffee and scrape in the seeds from the vanilla pod, then add the pod as well. Remove from the heat and leave to cool. Meanwhile, put the gelatine in a small pan, cover with cold water and leave to soak for 5 minutes. Heat gently until the gelatine has dissolved.

Take the vanilla pod out of the pan and stir in the rum, sieved ricotta and the gelatine. Strain through a fine sieve, then pour into 4 ramekins or similar moulds and chill for at least 2 hours, until set.

For the compote, put the sugar, water and lemon juice in a pan and bring slowly to the boil, stirring to dissolve the sugar. Reduce the heat, add the sliced apricots and poach for about 5 minutes, until just tender. Remove from the heat and leave to cool, then chill.

Turn out the coffee ricotta custards, or serve them in the ramekins if you prefer, accompanied by the apricot compote and decorated with sprigs of mint, if liked.

Nutritional value per serving:

Calories: 449

Fats: 24g

Carbohydrates: 48g

Salt: 0.22g

rhubarb in chilled syrup with cheese sorbet

350ml (12fl oz) red wine

4 tablespoons grenadine syrup

juice and zest of 1 orange

1 cinnamon stick

75g (3oz) caster sugar

750g (1lb 10oz) rhubarb, peeled and
    cut into 5cm (2in) lengths

Cheese sorbet

500ml (18fl oz) milk

175g (6oz) caster sugar

juice and zest of 1 small orange

175g (6oz) cream cheese

Nutritional value per serving:

Calories: 623

Fats: 23g

Carbohydrates: 88g

Salt: 0.68g

For the sorbet, put the milk, sugar, orange juice and zest in a pan and bring to the boil, stirring to dissolve the sugar, then remove from the heat and leave to cool. Stir this mixture into the cream cheese. Pour into an ice-cream maker and freeze until firm, following the manufacturer's instructions.

If you don't have an ice-cream maker, pour the mixture into a shallow container and put it in the freezer. After about 30 minutes, when the mixture is beginning to set, remove from the freezer and beat well with an electric beater or hand whisk to disperse any ice crystals, then return it to the freezer. Repeat this 2 or 3 times and then freeze until firm.

For the punch syrup, put the wine, grenadine syrup, orange juice and zest, cinnamon and sugar into a pan and boil until reduced by half its volume.

Add the rhubarb to the syrup and cook gently for up to 5 minutes, until the rhubarb is tender and sweet but still holds its shape. Transfer to a bowl and leave to cool, then chill thoroughly. Serve with scoops of the cheese sorbet.

TIP

For an interesting contrast, you could serve the rhubarb and punch syrup with the sorbet while they are still warm.

warming winter desserts

tamarind-baked winter fruits

1 vanilla pod, split open lengthways

150g (5oz) palm sugar (or demerara sugar)

2 lemongrass stalks, outer layers removed,
    tender inner core finely shredded

1$\frac{1}{2}$ teaspoons finely grated fresh root ginger

4 star anise

2 tablespoons tamarind paste

50g (2oz) unsalted butter

2 ripe pears, peeled, cored and quartered

6 ripe plums, halved and stoned

8 prunes, stoned

8 dried figs

12 dried apricots

100ml (3$\frac{1}{2}$fl oz) sweet white wine

juice of 1 lime

Preheat the oven to 190°C/375°F/gas mark 5. Combine the vanilla pod, sugar, lemongrass, ginger, star anise and tamarind in a pan with 150ml (1$\frac{1}{4}$ pints) of water, bring to the boil and simmer for 10 minutes. Remove from the heat and set aside.

Heat a casserole or deep, flameproof baking dish on the stove, add the butter, then add all the fruit and fry for 1-2 minutes, until lightly caramelised. Pour over the wine, lime juice and tamarind mixture and stir to coat the fruit. Place in the oven for 10-12 minutes, until the fruit is tender and lightly glazed. Serve warm.

Nutritional value per serving:

Calories: 515

Fats: 11g

Carbohydrates: 100g

Salt: 0.13g

grilled figs in coriander-lime syrup

1 bunch of coriander, leaves and stalks
    separated
juice from a 5cm (2in) piece of fresh
    root ginger (see below)
juice and grated zest of 2 limes
300ml (½ pint) Sauternes (or other
    sweet wine)
150ml (¼ pint) glucose syrup
4 green cardamom pods, split
12 ripe purple figs
1½ teaspoons vanilla sugar

Put the coriander stalks in a pan with the ginger juice, lime juice and zest, wine, glucose syrup and cardamom pods and bring gently to the boil. Reduce the heat and simmer for 5 minutes. Add the whole figs and poach gently for 3 minutes, then remove from the heat and leave to cool. Remove the figs from the syrup and set aside. Return the syrup to the heat and simmer until it begins to thicken. Meanwhile, blanch the coriander leaves in boiling water for a few seconds, then drain well and refresh in iced water. Drain and pat dry. Add the leaves to the hot syrup and leave for 2–3 minutes. Pour the mixture into a blender and blitz until smooth. Strain and leave to cool, then chill.

Cut the figs lengthways in half and place on a baking tray. Sprinkle with the vanilla sugar and place under a hot grill for 2–3 minutes, until caramelised. Arrange the figs on serving plates, drizzle over the syrup and serve.

How to make ginger juice

For natural ginger juice, grate a piece of ginger and squeeze through muslin. When grating you will find that the tougher fibres get caught in the grater; discard these.

Nutritional value per serving:

Calories: 264

Fats: 1g

Carbohydrates: 52g

Salt: 0.37g

caramelised banana tart

Base

75g (3oz) butter

45g (1½oz) soft brown (Barbados) sugar

45g (1½oz) caster sugar

4-5 bananas

a little freshly squeezed lemon juice

Topping

1 ripe banana, mashed

2 tablespoons crème fraîche

1 teaspoon pure vanilla essence

175g (6oz) caster sugar

75g (3oz) butter

2 eggs

175g (6oz) self-raising flour

Preheat the oven to 180°C/350°F/gas mark 4.

Melt the butter in a large flameproof and ovenproof sauté pan or heavy tin, add the sugars and stir well to dissolve. Slice the bananas and arrange in concentric circles over the base. Squeeze a little freshly squeezed lemon juice over the bananas.

Next make the topping. Mash the banana, add the crème fraîche and vanilla essence. Cream the butter, add the caster sugar and beat until light and fluffy. Add the eggs one at a time and continue to beat well. Gently fold in the flour and banana mixture alternately.

Spread the topping evenly and carefully over the bananas. Bake in the pre-heated oven for 45-50 minutes or until golden brown and fully cooked. Allow to rest in the dish for 5-10 minutes before turning out onto a warm serving plate so that the bananas are uppermost. Be careful of the hot juices.

Serve warm with softly whipped cream or crème fraîche.

Nutritional value per serving:

Calories: 578

Fats: 24 g

Carbohydrates: 89g

Salt: 0.83g

saffron pavlova with **lime curd**

6 egg whites

200g (7oz) caster sugar

4 pinches saffron powder

1 teaspoon white wine vinegar

1 teaspoon boiling water

½ teaspoon vanilla extract

1 tablespoon cornflour

double cream or plain yogurt, to serve

a little blanched shredded lime zest, to
   decorate

Lime curd

6 egg yolks

175g (6oz) caster sugar

juice and grated zest 6 large limes
   (you will need 175ml (6fl oz) juice)

pinch of salt

125g (4½oz) chilled unsalted butter, diced

Preheat the oven to 130°C/250°F/gas mark ½. Put the egg whites and sugar in a clean, dry bowl and whisk until they form stiff peaks. Mix the saffron powder with the vinegar and boiling water, then whisk it into the beaten whites with the vanilla extract. Finally fold in the cornflour.

Line 2 baking sheets with baking parchment and spread the meringue mixture on it in 6 mounded circles (alternatively, pipe the mixture into 6 nests, using a piping bag with a plain nozzle). Bake for 50-60 minutes, until they are crisp but still pale on the outside and have a soft marshmallow centre. Store in an airtight container until needed.

For the lime curd, beat the egg yolks and sugar together until thick and creamy, then add the lime juice and zest. Place in a heavy-based pan and cook, stirring, over a low heat until the mixture thickens a little. Add the salt and immediately remove from the heat. Whisk in the chilled diced butter and leave to cool. Cover and keep in the fridge until required.

To serve, top each saffron pavlova with a good dollop of lime curd and then pour over some cream or yogurt and decorate with a little blanched lime zest.

Nutritional value per serving:

Calories: 585

Fats: 32g

Carbohydrates: 69g

Salt: 0.42g

crêpes suzette

Batter
makes 8 pancakes
50g (2oz) plain flour
1 tablespoon oil
1 egg
1 egg yolk
2 teaspoons orange curaçao liqueur
150ml (¼ pint) milk

Sauce
grated rind of 225g (8oz) large ripe oranges
75g (3oz) softened butter
50g (2oz) caster sugar
generous tablespoon each of brandy
   and curaçao

First make the batter: put the flour in a bowl and make a well in the centre. Into this pour the oil, egg, egg yolk and orange curaçao. Stir, gradually drawing in the flour from the sides. Add the milk slowly until it is the consistency of thin cream. Set aside in the refrigerator for 30 minutes. Then make the crêpes by putting a small ladleful of batter at a time into a hot non-stick frying pan; as soon as bubbles rise to the surface, flip over and cook the other side. Keep the crêpes ready for use later.

For the sauce, add the rind of the oranges to the butter and sugar, and cream vigorously until smooth.

To finish: put the pan over a high heat. Melt about 10g (½oz) butter in it. When bubbling, put a cooked crêpe in and heat through, turning so that both sides get warm. Fold it into a fan shape and rest it against the side of the pan. Continue in the same way with the remaining pancakes. There should be enough to make 8 pancakes altogether. Sprinkle them with caster sugar. Pour over brandy and curaçao. Set alight, to burn off the alcohol, keeping your face away from the flames. Tilt the pan and spoon the juices over the pancakes until the flame subsides. Serve immediately on hot plates.

TIP
When cooked, crêpes may be stacked on top of each other and peeled apart later. Crêpes stored in this way may be kept in the fridge and used hours or even days later. They will peel off each other easily.

Nutritional value per serving:
Calories: 147
Fats: 6g
Carbohydrates: 16g
Salt: 0.06g

roasted pears in ginger butter

25g (1oz) caster sugar

2 tablespoons honey

2.5cm (1in) piece of fresh root ginger,
   finely grated

4 tablespoons white wine

2.5cm (1in) piece of cinnamon stick

4 ripe but firm pears, preferably Williams

50g (2oz) unsalted butter

2 tablespoons rum

1 teaspoon finely chopped preserved ginger

Put the sugar, honey, grated ginger, wine, cinnamon and 150ml ($1/4$ pint) of water in a pan and bring to the boil, stirring. Simmer until the syrup has reduced by half, then strain and set aside.

Peel and core the pears and cut them in half vertically, but leave the stalks on. Heat a large frying pan (big enough to take the 8 pear halves lying flat), add the butter and heat until it begins to foam. Add the pears, laying them flat around the pan, core-side down. Cook for 2-3 minutes, until golden underneath, then turn and cook the other side. Add the strained syrup and the rum to the pan and cover with a lid. Reduce the heat and leave the pears to caramelise in the buttery syrup, turning occasionally – this will take 4-5 minutes.

Arrange the pears on serving plates, add the preserved ginger to the syrup and pour it over the pears.

Nutritional value per serving:

Calories: 207

Fats: 10g

Carbohydrates: 23g

Salt: 0.01g

blue cheese and pecan pie

Pastry

350g (12oz) plain flour

225g (8oz) unsalted butter, cut into small pieces

pinch of salt

110g (4oz) icing sugar

finely grated zest of half a lemon

1 egg beaten

65g (2½oz) unsalted butter

4 tablespoons golden syrup

110g (4oz) mild blue cheese such as
    Cashel Blue, cut into small cubes

150g (5oz) soft brown sugar

3 eggs

2 tablespoons rum

½ teaspoon vanilla extract

pinch of salt

150g (5oz) pecan nuts

Preheat the oven to 190°C/375°F/gas mark 5. Sift the flour onto a work surface and make a well in the centre. Put the butter, salt, sugar and lemon zest in the well and add the egg. With your fingertips, gradually bring the flour into the centre until all the ingredients form a soft dough. Knead lightly for 1 minute, until smooth, then form into a ball. Wrap in cling film and chill for 2 hours. Roll out the pastry on a floured surface to 3mm (⅛in) thick and use to line a 23cm (9in) flan tin, 2.5cm (1in) deep. Bake blind for 10 minutes, then remove the paper and beans and bake for a further 5 minutes. Remove from the oven and reduce the temperature to 180°C/350°F/gas mark 4.

Heat the butter and golden syrup in a pan, add half the cheese and stir until melted. In a bowl, whisk together the sugar, eggs, rum, vanilla and salt. Add the pecan nuts and then stir into the syrup and cheese mixture. Add the remaining cheese and pour the mixture into the pastry case. Bake for about 30 minutes, until just set.

How to bake blind

Cut a circle of silicone paper and place over the pastry case. Fill with ceramic beans, as here, or use dried beans such as haricot or kidney beans, or even rice.

Nutritional value per serving:

Calories: 1557

Fats: 100g

Carbohydrates: 147g

Salt: 1.64g

SERVES 9

PREPARATION TIME: 10 MINUTES

COOKING TIME: 1 HOURS

CHILLING TIME: 1-2 HOURS

date crumble slice

125g (4½oz) butter, softened
50g (2oz) demerara sugar
1 egg yolk
50g (2oz) ground almonds
200g (7oz) plain flour
250g (9oz) chopped dates
125g (4½oz) cream cheese
1 teaspoon mixed spice
1 tablespoon demerara sugar
icing sugar, to dust
single cream or custard, to serve

Preheat the oven to 180°C/350°F/gas mark 4.

Prepare the dough. In a large bowl, or the bowl of a food processor, cream together the butter and demerara sugar, add the egg yolk and beat well. Fold in the ground almonds and flour. It may be necessary to work the mixture with your hands at this stage. It will look very dry but do not be tempted to add any liquid. After a short while it will easily come together into a ball. Wrap in cling film and chill until the dough is very firm. This will take 1-2 hours.

Place the chopped dates in a pan and cover with water. Bring to the boil and cook for 3 minutes. Turn off the heat and leave to stand for 5 minutes or until the dates are soft. Drain well.

Remove the dough from the refrigerator and cut in two. Using a coarse grater, grate half of the dough to cover the base of a 33 x 10cm (13 x 4in) rectangular or 23cm (9in) round tart tin. Press it down loosely. When cooked it will melt to form a base. Cover with an even layer of the dates. Spoon the cream cheese over the fruit and spread to cover. Grate the remaining dough over the top. Mix the spice and extra demerara sugar together, then sprinkle onto the tart. Bake for 35-40 minutes until golden brown.

Remove from the tin and dust with icing sugar before serving with single cream or custard.

Nutritional value per serving:
Calories: 433
Fats: 25g
Carbohydrates: 50g
Salt: 0.44g

parkin

100g (3½oz) plain flour

200g (7oz) medium oatmeal

25g (1oz) brown sugar

2.5cm (1in) piece of fresh root ginger,
   finely grated

pinch of ground ginger

pinch of salt

225g (8oz) golden syrup

100g (3½oz) unsalted butter

1 teaspoon bicarbonate of soda

4 tablespoons full-fat milk, warmed

Preheat the oven to 170°C/325°F/gas mark 3. Mix all the dry ingredients together in a large bowl. Place the syrup and butter in a saucepan and heat gently until the butter has melted. Dissolve the bicarbonate of soda in the warm milk, then pour both liquids into the flour mixture and stir well.

Pour into a greased and lined 20cm (8in) square cake tin and bake for 45-50 minutes; when it is done, a cocktail stick inserted in the centre should come out clean. Leave to cool in the tin, then turn out and cut into squares.

TIP

Store parkin in an airtight container; the longer you keep it, the stickier and better it will become.

Nutritional value per serving:

Calories: 449

Fats: 17g

Carbohydrates: 72g

Salt:1.22 g

vanilla & orange marmalade pudding

150g (5oz) caster sugar

150g (5oz) unsalted butter

1 teaspoon vanilla extract

3 eggs, separated

100g (3^1/$_2$oz) self-raising flour, sifted

4 tablespoons golden syrup

4 tablespoons good-quality orange marmalade

2 vanilla pods

Preheat the oven to 190°C/375°F/gas mark 5. In a bowl, beat 100g (3^1/$_2$oz) of the sugar with the butter until pale and creamy. Add the vanilla extract, then beat in the egg yolks one at a time. Fold in the flour. In a separate bowl, whisk the egg whites with the remaining sugar until they form stiff peaks. Stir a quarter of the whites into the egg yolk mixture to loosen it, then carefully fold in the rest.

Gently heat the golden syrup and marmalade together in a pan. Slit the vanilla pods open lengthways and scrape out the seeds with a small teaspoon or the point of a sharp knife. Add to the marmalade and syrup and mix well.

Grease eight ramekins and place 2 tablespoons of the vanilla marmalade in the base of each one. Top with the pudding mixture, filling them three-quarters full, and tap the ramekins to release any air pockets. Cover with foil and place in a roasting tin of hot water (the water should come halfway up the side of the ramekins). Place in the oven and bake for 40-45 minutes.

Run a knife around the edge of each pudding and turn out on to a serving plate. Serve with copious amounts of clotted cream or other cream.

Nutritional value per serving:

Calories: 325

Fats: 18g

Carbohydrates: 41g

Salt: 0.25g

tunisian orange cake

50g (2oz) slightly stale white breadcrumbs

200g (7oz) caster sugar

100g (3$^{1}/_{2}$oz) ground almonds

1$^{1}/_{2}$ level teaspoons baking powder

200ml (7fl oz) sunflower oil

4 eggs

zest of 1 large unwaxed orange, finely grated

zest of $^{1}/_{2}$ unwaxed lemon, finely grated

cream, Greek yogurt or crème fraîche, to serve

Citrus syrup

juice of 1 unwaxed orange

juice of $^{1}/_{2}$ unwaxed lemon

75g (3oz) sugar

2 cloves

1 cinnamon stick

Line the base of a 20.5cm (8in) round tin with a round of greaseproof paper. Grease and flour the tin. Mix the breadcrumbs with the sugar, almonds and baking powder. Whisk the oil with the eggs, pour into the dry ingredients and mix well. Add the orange and lemon zests. Pour the mixture into the prepared tin. Put into a cold oven, and turn on with the heat set to 180°C/350°F/gas mark 4.

Bake for 45-60 minutes or until the cake is golden brown. A skewer inserted into the centre should come out clean. Allow to cool for 5 minutes before turning out onto a plate.

Meanwhile make the citrus syrup. Put all the ingredients into a stainless-steel saucepan, bring gently to the boil, stirring until the sugar has dissolved completely. Simmer for 3 minutes. While the cake is still warm, pierce it with a skewer. Spoon the hot syrup over the cake. Leave to cool.

Spoon excess syrup back over the cake every now and then until it is all soaked up. You can remove the cloves and cinnamon stick or leave them on top of the cake for decoration. Serve with softly whipped cream or thick Greek yogurt.

Nutritional value per serving:

Calories: 640

Fats: 43g

Carbohydrates: 57g

Salt: 0.67g

coconut cassava cake

1.3kg (3lb) cassava, peeled and grated

1 large fresh coconut, grated

450g (1lb) white cheese (Cheddar is fine), grated

pinch of salt

2 egg yolks

250ml (a scant half pint) milk

225g (8oz) sugar

4 tablespoons softened butter

1 teaspoon aniseeds, lightly toasted and crushed

Place the cassava, the coconut and the cheese in a bowl. Add the remaining ingredients and mix together to make a smooth soft dough. Set it aside for an hour to swell.

Preheat the oven to 150°C/300°F/gas mark 2.

Transfer the dough to a buttered baking tin – a large loaf tin is perfect – and bake for an hour, until firm to the finger, well-risen and browned. Surprisingly light and moist – it is delicious with fresh pineapple.

Nutritional value per serving:

Calories: 836

Fats: 46g

Carbohydrates: 93g

Salt: 1.45g

plum pudding

175g (6oz) shredded beef suet (or use the
    vegetarian substitute)

175g (6oz) sugar

200g (7oz) soft breadcrumbs

225g (8oz) currants

225g (8oz) raisins

110g (4oz) candied peel

1-2 teaspoons mixed spice

pinch of salt

2 tablespoons flour

3 eggs

50ml (2fl oz) flesh of a baked apple

50ml (2fl oz) Irish whiskey

Brandy butter

75g (3oz) butter

75g (3oz) icing sugar

2-6 tablespoons brandy

Mix the dry ingredients thoroughly. Whisk the eggs and add them with the apple and whiskey. Stir very well indeed. Fill a pudding bowl. Cover with a round of greaseproof paper or a butter paper pressed down on top of the pudding. Put a large round of greaseproof or brown paper over the top of a 1.8 litre (3 pint) pudding bowl, tying it firmly under the rim. Place in a saucepan one-third full of boiling water and simmer for 10 hours. Do not allow the water to boil over the top and do not let it boil dry either. Store in a cool place until needed.

To make the brandy butter, cream the butter until very light, add the icing sugar and beat again. Then beat in the brandy, drop by drop. If you have a food processor, use it: you will get a wonderfully light and fluffy butter.

On Christmas day: boil for $1\frac{1}{2}$-2 hours before serving. Serve with brandy butter.

TIP

Leftover pudding may be fried in butter.

Nutritional value per serving:

Calories: 712

Fats: 30g

Carbohydrates: 105g

Salt: 1.02g

treacle pear pudding

25g (1oz) butter

2 heaped tablespoons golden syrup

1 pear

150g (5oz) butter, softened

150g (5oz) caster sugar

2 eggs, beaten

150g (5oz) self-raising flour

3 tablespoons cider or Perry

single cream, to serve

Use a little of the butter to grease a 1.2 litre (2 pint) pudding basin. Spoon the golden syrup into the base of the bowl. Peel, core and dice the pear and place on top of the syrup. Dot with the remaining butter.

Cream the butter and sugar until light and fluffy. Incorporate the eggs little by little, beating well between each addition. Sift the flour and fold in, adding enough cider to give a firm dropping consistency. Spoon the mixture into the pudding basin on top of the fruit. Cover with a disc of buttered greaseproof paper. Cut a circle of foil that will overhang the top of the basin by 7.5cm (3in). Make a 1cm (½in) pleat in the foil then place it over the basin and tie securely with string. The pleat allows for expansion during cooking.

Stand the basin on a trivet in a deep pan. Add enough water to come 5cm (2in) up the sides of the bowl. Cover with a tightly fitting lid and steam for 1-1½ hours. To test if the pudding is cooked, remove the foil and greaseproof paper disc and insert a small skewer into the centre; it should come out clean. If not cooked, re-cover the basin and steam for a little longer. If cooked ahead of time, turn off the heat and leave until required.

Lift the pudding from the pan, snip the string and remove the foil and the greaseproof paper disc. Invert the basin onto a serving dish. Serve with single cream or cinnamon custard.

TIP

If you prefer the topping of your pudding to be sticky rather than syrupy, add a couple of tablespoons of fresh breadcrumbs on top of the golden syrup before adding the fruit. This absorbs some of the liquid and gives a more traditional treacle pudding texture.

Nutritional value per serving:

Calories: 468

Fats: 26g

Carbohydrates: 57g

Salt: 0.93g

pumpkin and ricotta torte with pine nuts

450g (1lb) slice of pumpkin, deseeded and
   sliced into wedges

3 tablespoons water

310g (11oz) sweet shortcrust pastry

500g (1lb 2oz) ricotta cheese

75ml (3fl oz) sour cream

3 eggs

200g (7oz) caster sugar

1 rounded tablespoon flour

50g (2oz) pine nuts

icing sugar, to dust

Preheat the oven to 180°C/350°F/gas mark 4. Place the pumpkin wedges in a roasting tin with 3 tablespoons of water, cover with a sheet of kitchen foil and bake for 1-1½ hours until completely tender. Cool, then remove the skin and process the flesh in a food processor until smooth.

Grease the sides of a 22cm (8½in) springform tin. This will help to hold the pastry in place. Use three-quarters of the pastry to line the prepared tin, pressing the dough well into the base and sides. Chill. Roll the remaining pastry to form a rectangle and cut into long strips about 1cm (½in) wide. Lay on a tray and chill whilst preparing the filling.

In a large bowl beat together the ricotta cheese and the pumpkin purée until smooth. Stir in the sour cream. Beat the eggs, then add to the purée mixture with the caster sugar and flour. Blend well together. Pour or spoon into the pastry case and sprinkle the pine nuts over the top.

Brush the pastry edge with a little water or egg white, then lay the chilled strips of pastry over the torte in a lattice pattern. Trim off the ends and bake for 45-55 minutes. The filling will rise and the crust will have a gorgeous golden colour. Switch off the oven and leave the torte to cool inside.

Remove from the tin and dust with icing sugar.

Nutritional value per serving:

Calories: 473

Fats: 26g

Carbohydrates: 50g

Salt: 0.39g

rhubarb crumble with vanilla cream

450g (1lb) plain flour, sifted

pinch of salt

225g (8oz) unsalted butter, cut into cubes

225g (8oz) caster sugar

1.3kg (3lb) fresh rhubarb

250g (9oz) caster sugar

finely grated zest and juice of 2 medium-sized
   oranges

Vanilla cream

600ml (1 pint) double cream

25g (1oz) icing sugar

1 vanilla pod, split lengthways, deseeded

Preheat the oven to 190°C/375°F/gas mark 5.

In an electric mixer, add the flour, salt, butter and the 225g (8oz) sugar. Mix until the texture resembles fine breadcrumbs.

Wash the rhubarb, and trim top and bottom. Cut the rhubarb into 5cm (2in) long pieces. Mix with the 250g (9oz) sugar, orange zest and juice, then place in an ovenproof dish. Cover the dish with foil, and bake for 30 minutes until the rhubarb is soft but still retains its shape.

Turn down the oven to 170°C/330°F/gas mark 3.

Divide the rhubarb and crumble topping between the serving dishes you are using. Bake for about 30 minutes, until you start to see the liquid bubbling out and the crumble is golden brown. While it cooks, prepare the cream.

Place the chilled cream in a mixing bowl, then add the icing sugar and vanilla. Whisk, by hand or with an electric mixer, until the mixture begins to thicken. If using an electric mixer, do not leave unattended, otherwise you could over-beat the cream and turn it into butter. The vanilla cream is best served as soon as it is made, which takes only a few minutes.

Nutritional value per serving:

Calories: 803

Fats: 48g

Carbohydrates: 92g

Salt: 0.28g

wicked &
wonderful

hazelnut praline

150ml (^{1}/$_4$ pint) single cream

100g (3^1/$_2$oz) white chocolate

100g (3^1/$_2$oz) hazelnut nougat (available in
specialist shops)

2 teaspoons pâté noisette (available in
specialist shops)

1 gelatine leaf, soaked in a small amount of
water

225ml (8fl oz) whipping cream, lightly whipped
ice cream and chocolate curls,
to serve

finely chopped hazelnuts, to serve

Put the cream in a pan and bring to the boil. Boil for 1-2 minutes, then add the white chocolate. When it starts to melt mix in the nougat and pâté noisette. Take off the heat and allow to cool slightly, then add the gelatine as the mixture starts to cool down.

Fold in the whipped cream. Pour into dariole moulds and freeze until set. To remove from the moulds, dip the base in boiling water for 10 seconds and then invert on to a plate. Serve with vanilla, chocolate or white chocolate ice cream and chocolate curls. Sprinkle with finely chopped hazelnuts.

Nutritional value per serving:

Calories: 587

Fats: 47g

Carbohydrates: 37g

Salt: 0.25g

hot **chocolate** fondants

250g (9oz) unsalted butter, plus extra for
   greasing

40g (1^1/$_2$oz) cocoa powder, plus extra for dusting

250g (9oz) plain chocolate (70 per cent
   cocoa solids)

120g (4^1/$_2$oz) plain flour

2 eggs

200g (7oz) caster sugar

Grease 6 x 200ml (7fl oz) dariole moulds with a little butter and then dust with cocoa powder. Set aside. Break the chocolate into pieces and place in a large heatproof bowl set over a pan of simmering water. Allow to melt and then gradually whisk in the butter. Set aside and allow to cool a little.

Sieve the plain flour and cocoa powder into a bowl. Whisk the eggs and sugar in another bowl until pale and fluffy, then fold into the cooled chocolate mixture until well combined. Finally fold in the flour mixture and either pipe or spoon into the prepared dariole moulds until each one is no more than three-quarters full, gently tapping to remove any air bubbles. Cover with cling film and chill for at least 3 hours or up to 5 hours.

Preheat the oven to 200°C/400°F/gas mark 6. Arrange the dariole moulds on a baking sheet and bake for 12-14 minutes. Leave to rest for a minute or two, then invert each dariole mould into the middle of a wide-rimmed bowl and serve immediately with a spoonful of whipped cream and some warmed chocolate sauce, if liked.

TIP

These chocolate fondants can be made well in advance, as they improve if they have been allowed to rest for at least three hours before baking.

Nutritional value per serving:

Calories: 487

Fats: 57g

Carbohydrates: 67g

Salt: 0.21g

bitter chocolate sorbet with raspberries

150g (5oz) caster sugar

40g (1^1/$_2$oz) liquid glucose

100ml (3^1/$_2$fl oz) milk

40g (1^1/$_2$oz) cocoa powder (good quality)

100g (3^1/$_2$oz) plain chocolate (70 per cent
    cocoa solids), finely chopped

450g (1lb) fresh raspberries

Place the caster sugar in a heavy-based pan with 400ml (14fl oz) of water, the liquid glucose, milk and cocoa powder. Bring to the boil, stirring from time to time, then simmer for 2 minutes, whisking constantly to prevent the bottom of the pan from catching.

Remove the pan from the heat and add the chocolate, stirring until the chocolate has melted. Pass through a fine sieve into a jug, cover with cling film and chill for a few hours until it is really cold.

Now you can either churn the mixture in an ice-cream machine or pour it into a plastic container and freeze until it is almost firm. If doing the latter, scrape the mixture into a food processor and whizz until smooth. Pour it back into the plastic container and repeat one more time. Return the sorbet to the freezer and freeze until firm.

To serve, quickly dip two tablespoons into boiling water and use to shape the sorbet into quenelles. Arrange three in each wide rimmed serving bowl and decorate with the raspberries. Serve immediately.

Nutritional value per serving:

Calories: 372

Fats: 13g

Carbohydrates: 63g

Salt: 0.32g

SERVES 4-6

PREPARATION TIME: 15 MINUTES

COOKING TIME: 45 MINUTES

FREEZING TIME: 1-3 HOURS

white chocolate & basil profiteroles with hot dark chocolate sauce

White chocolate and basil ice cream

10 basil leaves, leaves and stalks separated

200ml (7fl oz) double cream

200ml (7fl oz) full-fat milk

200g (7oz) white chocolate, broken into pieces

4 egg yolks

25g (1oz) caster sugar

Choux pastry

200ml (7fl oz) full-fat milk

60g (2^1/$_2$oz) unsalted butter, diced

20g (^{3}/$_4$oz) caster sugar

125g (4^1/$_2$oz) plain flour

4 eggs

1 egg yolk, beaten with 2 tablespoons milk

2 tablespoons flaked almonds

Chocolate sauce

100g (3^1/$_2$oz) good-quality dark chocolate

^{1}/$_2$ tablespoon caster sugar

75ml (3fl oz) double cream

small knob of butter

Nutritional value per serving:

Calories: 1237

Fats: 93g

Carbohydrates: 82g

Salt: 0.59g

To make the ice cream, put the basil stalks in a saucepan with the cream and milk, bring gently to the boil and simmer for 1 minute. Add the white chocolate, stir well, then remove from the heat and infuse for 10 minutes. In a bowl, whisk together the egg yolks and sugar until creamy. Strain the basil-infused cream on to the egg yolks, whisking constantly, then return to the pan and cook, stirring, over a low heat, until the mixture thickens (do not let it boil). Remove from the heat and leave to cool. Stir in the torn basil leaves, pour into an ice-cream machine and freeze.

Next make the choux pastry. Preheat the oven to 200°C/400°F/gas mark 6. Put the milk, butter and sugar in a pan. As soon as it comes to the boil, rain in the flour and beat with a wooden spoon until the mixture leaves the sides of the pan clean. Allow to cool slightly, then beat in the eggs one by one to give a thick, glossy mixture.

Lightly oil a baking sheet and sprinkle it with a little water. Fit a pastry bag with a 2.5cm (1in) plain nozzle and pipe out walnut-sized mounds of the choux pastry, brush with a little beaten egg wash and sprinkle over the flaked almonds. Bake for 15 minutes, then open the oven door slightly and leave for a further 10 minutes so that they dry out. Remove from the oven, pierce each profiterole with a skewer so the steam can escape, then leave to cool.

For the chocolate sauce, place all the ingredients in a pan and bring gently to the boil, then whisk until smooth, adding a little boiling water if it is too thick. To serve, cut each profiterole in half horizontally, fill with a ball of the ice cream and top with the lid. Arrange on serving plates and pour the hot chocolate sauce over and around.

velvet chocolate mousse with mint glass biscuits

375ml (13fl oz) double cream

350ml (12fl oz) full-fat milk

6 egg yolks

125g (4$\frac{1}{2}$oz) caster sugar

2 gelatine leaves

375g (13oz) good-quality dark chocolate (at
    least 70 per cent cocoa solids), chopped

Mint glass biscuits

2 tablespoons mint leaves,
    blanched for 10 seconds and dried

100g (3$\frac{1}{2}$oz) unsalted butter

100ml (3$\frac{1}{2}$fl oz) golden syrup

50ml (2fl oz) crème de menthe

200g (7oz) caster sugar

100g (3$\frac{1}{2}$oz) plain flour

Nutritional value per serving:

Calories: 1775

Fats: 106g

Carbohydrates: 190g

Salt: 0.72g

Bring the cream and milk to the boil in a pan. In a separate bowl, whisk together the egg yolks and sugar until light and creamy. Whisking constantly, pour in the cream and milk and stir well. Return to the pan and cook, stirring, over a low heat, until the mixture is thick enough to coat the back of the spoon. Remove from the heat. Cover the gelatine leaves with cold water and leave to soak for 5 minutes. Drain well, squeezing out excess water, and add to the custard mixture. Stir well to dissolve the gelatine.

Place the chocolate in a bowl, pour over the hot custard and leave to melt, stirring occasionally. When the chocolate has melted, strain the mixture through a fine sieve into a bowl. Leave to cool, cover with cling film and chill for at least 4 hours, until set.

To make the biscuits, chop the blanched mint leaves finely and set aside. Put the butter, golden syrup and crème de menthe in a pan and heat gently until the butter has melted. Mix the sugar and flour together in a bowl, then pour in the syrup mixture, add the mint and stir well to form a paste. Cover with cling film and chill for 1 hour, until very cold.

Preheat the oven to 180°C/350°F/gas mark 4. Remove the biscuit mixture from the fridge and shape into 12 balls, 2.5cm (1in) in diameter. Place them well spaced out on two baking sheets lined with baking parchment and press each one out to form a small disc. Bake for 8-10 minutes, until pale golden, then remove from the oven and leave to cool and crisp up. Store in a sealed container until ready to use.

To serve, layer the biscuits with the chocolate mousse.

hot chocolate mousse

50g (2oz) butter, melted

70g (2^1/$_2$oz) caster sugar

250g (9oz) extra-bitter chocolate (70 per cent
   cocoa solids)

125g (4^1/$_2$oz) butter

8 eggs, separated

180g (6^1/$_2$oz) caster sugar

50g (2oz) plain flour, sieved

75g (3oz) extra-bitter chocolate, chopped into
   small pieces

icing sugar, to dust

250g (9oz) clotted cream

Preheat the oven to 160°C/325°F/gas mark 3.

Brush the insides of six small teacups with melted butter and coat with caster sugar.

Cut the chocolate and butter into 2.5cm (1in) pieces, then place in a metal bowl over a pan of barely simmering water to melt. Do not allow the chocolate to get too hot as this will make it difficult to combine with the other ingredients. In an electric mixer, whisk the egg whites on a high speed until foamy. Add the caster sugar gradually, continuing to whisk until the consistency is smooth, glossy and stiff. Remove the chocolate from the heat, add the egg yolks and mix thoroughly. Fold in the egg whites and add the sieved flour. Continue to fold until all the ingredients are well combined. Remove the cups from the refrigerator. Divide the extra chopped chocolate pieces between them. Spoon the mousse mixture into the cups until each is three-quarters full.

Boil a kettle of water. Put the mousses into a deep roasting tin, then pour boiling water into the tin to halfway up the moulds. Cook the mousses for about 20 minutes or until well risen above the edge of the moulds.

Carefully remove the tea cups from the water – remembering they will be hot. Place them on a clean tea towel to drain away any excess water. Dust with icing sugar and serve with a spoonful of clotted cream on the side.

Nutritional value per serving:

Calories: 463

Fats: 38g

Carbohydrates: 28g

Salt: 0.3g

lemon tart

450g (15oz) butter

225g (8oz) sugar

700g (1¼ lb) self-raising flour

2 eggs

Filling

1 litre (1¾ pints) double cream

zest and juice of 7 lemons

200g (7oz) sugar

10 egg yolks

Preheat the oven to 160°C/325°F/gas mark 3.

To make the pastry, combine the butter, sugar and flour together in a food processor. Add the eggs and mix to make a smooth dough. Wrap the dough in cling film and chill for at least 30 minutes before using.

Roll out the pastry and use to line one 30cm (12in) greased flan dish, or 4 individual flan tins. Transfer to the freezer for 20 minutes. Bake straight from the freezer for 10 minutes, or until golden brown. Remove from the oven and leave to cool. Reduce the oven temperature to 100°C/225°F/gas mark ¼.

To make the filling, bring the cream and lemon zest to the boil in a pan. Combine the sugar, egg yolks and lemon juice in a bowl. Whisk the cream mixture into the egg mixture, combining thoroughly. Strain the filling into the tart shell and bake for 20-30 minutes.

Nutritional value per serving:

Calories: 1210

Fats: 74g

Carbohydrates: 128g

Salt: 1.12g

chocolate **almond** gâteau

110g (4oz) best-quality dark chocolate

2 tablespoons red Jamaica rum

110g (4oz) whole almonds

110g (4oz) butter, preferably unsalted

110g (4oz) caster sugar

3 eggs, separated

1 tablespoon caster sugar

50g (2oz) plain white flour

50g (2oz) whole almonds or best quality
    ground almonds, blanched and peeled

Chocolate icing

110g (4oz) best quality dark chocolate

2 tablespoons red Jamaica rum

110g (4oz) unsalted butter

To decorate

crystallised violets

toasted flaked almonds

Nutritional value per serving:

Calories: 607

Fats: 47g

Carbohydrates: 36g

Salt: 0.34g

Preheat the oven to 180°C/350°F/gas mark 4.

Grease 2 x 18cm (7in) sandwich tins and line the base of each with greaseproof paper. Melt the chocolate with the rum on a very gentle heat. Grind the almonds in a food processor; they should still be slightly gritty.

Cream the butter, and then add the caster sugar, beating until light and fluffy. Beat in the egg yolks one by one. Whisk the egg whites with a pinch of salt until stiff. Add 1 tablespoon of caster sugar and continue to whisk until they reach the stiff peak stage. Add the melted chocolate to the butter and sugar mixture and then add the almonds. Fold in a quarter of the egg white mixture followed by a quarter of the sieved flour. Fold in the remaining egg white mixture and flour alternately until they have all been added.

Divide the mixture between the two prepared tins and make a hollow in the centre of each cake. Bake in the oven for 19-25 minutes.

IMPORTANT: The cake should be slightly underdone in the centre. Sides should be cooked but the centre a little unset. Allow to cool for a few minutes in the tins, turn out gently onto a wire rack, remove the paper and allow to get cold.

For the icing, melt the chocolate with the rum in a Pyrex bowl over a low heat. Beat in the unsalted butter a tablespoon at a time. Beat occasionally until cool. If the icing liquefies, put it into the fridge to firm up, then whisk until stiff.

When the cake is completely cold, fill and ice with the mixture. Pipe any remaining icing around the top and decorate with flaked almonds and crystallised violets.

brownies

50g (2oz) best quality dark chocolate

100g (3$\frac{1}{2}$oz) butter

200g (7oz) caster sugar

2 eggs, lightly whisked

$\frac{1}{2}$ teaspoon vanilla extract

75g (3oz) white flour

$\frac{1}{2}$ teaspoon baking powder

pinch salt

110g (4oz) chopped walnuts

Preheat the oven to 180°C/350°F/gas mark 4.

Melt the chocolate in a bowl over a pan of gently simmering water or in a low oven. Cream the butter and sugar and beat in the eggs, vanilla extract and melted chocolate. Lastly stir in the flour, baking powder, salt and chopped nuts. Spread the mixture into a 20.5cm (8in) square tin and bake in the oven for about 30–35 minutes. Cut into 5cm (2in) squares for serving.

Nutritional value per serving:

Calories: 185

Fats: 12g

Carbohydrates: 18g

Salt: 0.25g

coffee granita

1 litre (1³⁄₄ pints) freshly made espresso coffee

5 tablespoons sugar

200ml (7fl oz) whipping cream

Put the coffee and sugar in a saucepan and gently heat until the sugar has dissolved – you may need more sugar to taste, so check. Remember, too, that because it is to be eaten chilled, the sweetness will be less pronounced.

Pour into a plastic tray and freeze, stirring every hour, so the crystals don't get too big.

To serve, remove the tray from the freezer about 40 minutes before serving. Break up with a wooden spoon and place in 6-8 iced long-stemmed glasses. Whip the cream, add to the glasses and serve.

Nutritional value per serving:

Calories: 177

Fats: 13g

Carbohydrates: 15g

Salt: 0.04g

chocolate tart with curled chocolate ganache

200g (7oz) flour

150g (5oz) caster sugar

150g (5oz) unsalted butter, cubed and at
    room temperature

40g (1½oz) cocoa powder

2 large eggs

25g (¾oz) dark chocolate

icing sugar, for dusting

ice cream and raspberry coulis, to serve (optional)

Filling

500g (1lb 2oz) dark chocolate

200ml (7fl oz) milk

350ml (12fl oz) double cream

1 vanilla pod, split

3 eggs

Ganache

250g (9oz) dark chocolate

50g (2oz) unsalted butter

250 ml (9fl oz) double cream

1 tablespoon brandy

Nutritional value per serving:

Calories: 989

Fats: 70g

Carbohydrates: 82g

Salt: 0.31g

Sift the flour into a mixing bowl and add the sugar, butter and cocoa. Blend together, add the eggs and mix to a firm paste. Chill for 1 hour, then grate the pastry into a flan tin evenly over the base and press down all over to form the base and sides of the tart shell. Finely grate over the dark chocolate and chill for about 20 minutes.

Preheat the oven to 180°C/350°F/gas mark 4. Melt the chocolate gently in a bowl over a pan of simmering water. In a separate pan, bring the milk, cream and split vanilla pod to a gentle simmer, then turn the heat to low. Crack the eggs into a large heatproof bowl and whisk lightly. Pull the milk and cream from heat. Continue to whisk the eggs while you pour in the milk and cream. Gently fold the melted chocolate into this mixture.

Remove the tart shell from the fridge, pour in the filling and place straight into the oven. After 5 minutes, turn the oven down to 150°C/300°F/gas mark 2, cook for 10 minutes more, then turn the oven down to 110°C/230°F/gas mark ¼ and cook for a further 20 minutes. Finally turn the oven off but leave the tart in there for about 25 minutes or so. Remove when cool.

Make the ganache: melt the chocolate in a bowl set over a saucepan of gently simmering water. Once it has melted, stir in the butter, remove from the heat and allow to cool for at least 20 minutes. Whip the double cream until just peaking and then mix in the brandy. Fold the cream gently into the cooled chocolate mixture, pour the mixture into a deep-sided baking tray about 20 x 40cm (8 x 16in) and place in the fridge to set for about 20 minutes. Once the ganache has set, drag a dessertspoon along the top to form curls (one for each serving) and place on top of the tart. Dust with icing sugar to serve.

ginger tiramisu

10 large eggs, separated
500g (1lb 2oz) caster sugar
10 tablespoons boiling water
350g (12oz) plain flour
5 teaspoons baking powder
pinch of salt

2 tablespoons jasmine tea
300ml ($^{1}/_{2}$ pint) boiling water
1 tablespoon caster sugar
125ml (4fl oz) ginger wine
1 tablespoon syrup from the crystallised ginger
finely grated rind of 1 orange

600g (1lb 4oz) mascarpone cheese
6 egg yolks
100g (3$^{1}/_{2}$oz) caster sugar
50ml (2fl oz) orange juice, strained
50ml (2fl oz) ginger wine
75g (3oz) crystallised ginger, cut into small dice
6 egg whites
300ml ($^{1}/_{2}$ pint) double cream

Nutritional value per serving:
Calories: 965
Fats: 54g
Carbohydrates: 105g
Salt: 1.38g

Preheat the oven to 180°C/350°F/gas mark 4. Grease and line two 28 x 35cm (11 x 14in) Swiss roll tins with baking parchment. Whisk the egg yolks and sugar in a mixer until light and creamy. Add the boiling water slowly and continue to whisk for a further 5 minutes. In a bowl, whisk the egg whites until they form soft peaks. Sift together the flour, baking powder and salt. With a metal spoon gently fold in the egg yolks then the egg whites, half at a time until well incorporated. Divide the mixture between the two tins. Cook for 20 minutes or until golden brown and springy to the touch. Remove from the oven and cool on a wire rack. When cool, cut the sponge in half lengthways, then cut 30 discs from it using a cutter slightly smaller than the glasses. The discs should be about 7mm ($^{1}/_{4}$in) thick.

Infuse the jasmine tea in the boiling water for about 30 minutes. Add the sugar, ginger wine, ginger syrup and orange zest.

Remove the mascarpone from the refrigerator $^{1}/_{2}$ hour before you need to use it. Whisk the egg yolks in a mixer with 75g (2$^{1}/_{2}$oz) of sugar, until light in colour and a thick consistency. Add the mascarpone, orange juice, ginger wine and pieces of crystallized ginger. Whisk until creamy and smooth. Whisk the egg whites with the remaining sugar until they form stiff glossy peaks. Whip the double cream gently. Gently fold the egg whites, then the cream, into the mascarpone mixture. Mix in well.

Place 1 disc in the base of each mould, brush with soaking liquid then put 1 tablespoon mascarpone mixture on top of each. Repeat for all the sponge discs, finishing with the mascarpone mixture on top. Level off the tops with a palette knife. Cover and chill.

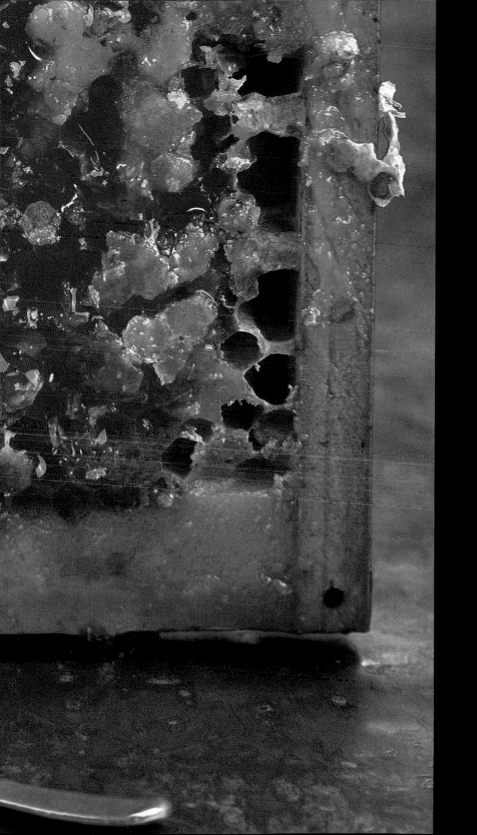

petit
fours

chocolate truffles

175g (6oz) best quality dark chocolate

50g (2oz) unsweetened chocolate

1 tablespoon Jamaica rum

75g (3oz) unsalted butter

2 tablespoons cream

75g (3oz) praline, finely crushed

melted chocolate and unsweetened cocoa
   powder for finishing

Melt the chocolate over a gentle heat to a thick cream with the rum. Draw aside, stir in the butter bit by bit, then add the cream and praline. Put small teaspoonfuls onto waxed or greaseproof paper. When set, have the melted chocolate ready. Put a little on the palms of the hands and lightly roll the truffles between them. Toss into a bowl of unsweetened cocoa powder. Brush off the surplus and put on racks to dry.

Nutritional value per serving:

Calories: 98

Fats: 7g

Carbohydrates: 7g

Salt: 0.05g

How to make chocolate truffles

stuffed dates

150g (6oz) peeled pistachio nuts (reserve 1 nut for each date)

1-2 tablespoons fragrant honey

50g (2oz) ground almonds

25-30 fresh dates (approximately 3-4 per person), stones removed

2 teaspoons orange blossom or rosewater

Place the pistachios and honey in a food processor and process at high speed until coarsely ground.

Transfer the content to a mixing bowl. Add the ground almonds and mix well. If the mixture is too loose add some more ground almonds.

Stuff a little of the mixture into each date, and decorate with a pistachio nut. Either arrange on individual serving plates on a pool of thick cream or serve in paper cases as petit fours.

Nutritional value per serving:
Calories: 83
Fats: 4g
Carbohydrates: 9g
Salt: 0.01g

halva

350g (12oz) caster sugar
pinch of saffron strands
2 cinnamon sticks
1 teaspoon ground cardamom
225ml (8fl oz) olive oil
350g (12oz) semolina
75g (3oz) flaked almonds
125ml (4fl oz) honey
2 tablespoons whole blanched almonds
1 teaspoon ground cinnamon

Place the sugar and saffron in a pan with 600ml (1 pint) of water and bring slowly to the boil, stirring from time to time to dissolve the sugar. Add the cinnamon and cardamom, simmer for 5 minutes, then remove from the heat and leave to infuse.

Meanwhile, in a separate pan, heat the olive oil until quite hot, stir in the semolina, reduce the heat and simmer for 20 minutes, until lightly golden. Add the flaked almonds and cook for 2 minutes. Strain in the saffron syrup and boil together for 5 minutes. Add the honey, remove from the heat and allow to cool slightly. Pour into a greased and lined shallow tin, about 25 x 20cm (10 x 8in), smooth the top and set aside to cool. Cut into small squares, top each one with a blanched almond and dust with the ground cinnamon.

Nutritional value per serving:
Calories: 136
Fats: 7g
Carbohydrates: 19g
Salt: 0.01g

coconut custard

225g (8oz) granulated sugar

250ml (9fl oz) thick coconut milk

1 teaspoon rosewater

$^{1}/_{2}$ teaspoon salt

3 eggs, lightly beaten (use whites only, if you
  have some to use up)

Place the sugar and coconut milk in a large pan and heat gently, stirring until the sugar has dissolved. Stir in the rosewater and salt. Add the beaten eggs (or egg whites) and fold in carefully.

Pour the resulting custard into a heatproof bowl or metal baking tray. Place in the top of a preheated steamer and cook for 30 minutes, or until set. Cut into small squares 2.5-4cm (1-1$^{1}/_{2}$in).

Nutritional value per serving:

Calories: 377

Fats: 14g

Carbohydrates: 61g

Salt: 0.94g

cherry tarts

Almond pastry

175g (6oz) plain flour

50g (2oz) ground almonds

1 tablespoon caster sugar

1/2 teaspoon salt

150g (5oz) butter

3 tablespoons cold water

450g (1lb) cherries, stoned (squeeze through
the stalk end)

4-6 tablespoons caster sugar (depending on the
cherries' acidity)

juice of an orange and a lemon

1 teaspoon cornflour mixed with a little water

2-3 tablespoons custard or soured cream

Toss the flour with the ground almonds, sugar and salt in a bowl. Cut the butter into the flour with a knife and then rub it in lightly with your fingertips until the mixture looks like fine breadcrumbs. Sprinkle in the water and press into a firm smooth ball of dough, still using your fingertips. Put the pastry aside to rest in a plastic bag in a cool place for 30 minutes to swell and gain elasticity.

Preheat the oven to 220°C/425°F/gas mark 7.

Roll the pastry out with a floured rolling pin – use small light movements: the pastry is fragile. Use a wine glass or pastry cutter to cut rounds of the right size for your tartlet tins. Place the pastry rounds in the tins and prick the bases with a fork to prevent any bubbles forming. Bake for 15-20 minutes – the almond pastry will first whiten and then turn golden. Remove to a baking rack to crisp and cool.

Meanwhile, put the stoned cherries in a pan with the sugar and the juices diluted with their own volume of water. Bring to the boil, turn down the heat and simmer for 10-15 minutes, until the cherries are tender. Remove with a slotted spoon and reserve. Allow the syrup to cool a little, then stir in the cornflour, reheat and bubble up for a moment to thicken.

Put a teaspoonful of the custard or cream into the base of each tartlet, arrange a few cherries on the top and finish with the thickened syrup.

Nutritional value per serving:

Calories: 250

Fats: 22g

Carbohydrates: 35g

Salt: 0.56g

guava cheese

900kg (2lb) guavas
450g (1lb) golden cane sugar

Rinse and roughly chop the guavas – skins, pips and all – and put them in a roomy saucepan with enough water to cover. Bring to the boil and cook for 20 minutes, until the fruit is soft and mushy. Dump the contents of the pan in a clean jelly-cloth and hang on a hook set over a bowl. Leave to drip overnight. Push the pulp through a sieve, discarding the skins and pips.

Put the sieved pulp in a pan and beat in the sugar. Cook very, very gently for at least an hour until the pulp and sugar have formed a soft, dark, dryish mass, or spread on a baking tray and leave in the lowest possible oven overnight. It'll set to a firm paste as it cools.

TIP
Wrap in paper and keep in a warm dry place - never in the fridge. Delicious with cheese.

Nutritional value per serving:
Calories: 20
Fats: 0g
Carbohydrates: 5g
Salt: 0g

brandy snap baskets

110g (4oz) butter

110g (4oz) caster sugar

4 tablespoons golden syrup

110g (4oz) white flour

juice of ½ lemon

large pinch of ground ginger

clean small jars to use as moulds

Preheat the oven to 180°C/350°F/gas mark 4. Line a baking sheet with silicone paper. Gently melt the butter with the caster sugar and golden syrup in a pan, take off the heat and stir in the sieved flour, lemon juice and ginger. Allow to cool. Drop generous tablespoonfuls of the mixture onto the tray spaced well apart. They should spread into a 12.5-15cm (5-6in) circle. Bake for 5-6 minutes or lacy and golden. Have the jars upturned ready to use as moulds. Leave the brandy snap baskets to cool for a minute or so, then lift quickly off the tray with an egg slice. Shape over the upturned jars to form baskets. Cool on a wire rack. Do one tray at a time or they will harden before you have time to shape them.

TIP

Fill with sliced bananas, butterscotch sauce and caramel ice cream, or with whipped cream and fresh fruit in season.

How to make brandy snaps

Roll the warm biscuits round the handle of a wooden spoon to make brandy snaps rather than baskets. Eat as they are or fill with whipped cream.

Nutritional value per serving:

Calories: 150

Fats: 8g

Carbohydrates: 21g

Salt: 0.21g

coffee kisses

350g (12oz) plain flour
110g (4oz) clarified butter, softened (see TIP)
110g (4oz) brown sugar
1 medium egg
2 tablespoons very strong black coffee
coffee beans to decorate

Sieve the flour with a pinch of salt. Beat the butter and sugar until light and fluffy, then beat in the egg forked up with the coffee. Work in the flour to make a ball of soft dough – you may need a little more flour. Cover with cling film and leave to rest in the fridge for an hour to firm up.

Heat the oven to 220°C/425°F/gas mark 7. On a lightly floured board, roll out the dough. Cut out rounds and arrange on a buttered baking sheet, allowing plenty of space for them to spread. Dampen the coffee beans and pop one on each biscuit. Bake for 20-25 minutes until golden. Transfer to a baking rack while still soft and warm – they crisp as they cool.

TIP
Clarified butter, though not essential, gives a crisper result. To clarify butter, warm till it liquefies, then pour off the oil, leaving the milky residue behind.

Nutritional value per serving:
Calories: 121
Fats: 6g
Carbohydrates: 17g
Salt: 0.01g

brazil nut cookies

110g (4oz) brazil nuts

110g (4oz) plain flour

1 heaped tablespoon cocoa powder

1/2 teaspoon baking powder

1/2 teaspoon salt

110g (4oz) softened unsalted butter

110g (4oz) brown sugar

1 egg, forked to blend

Reserve 18 of the best brazil nuts. Crush the rest to a coarse powder and toss with the flour sieved with the cocoa, baking powder and salt.

Beat the butter with the sugar till light and pale. Beat in the egg, then the flour and nuts. The mixture should be soft enough to drop from the spoon, so you may need a little milk.

Preheat the oven to 190°C/375°F/gas mark 4. Butter a baking sheet and sprinkle lightly with flour. Drop spoonfuls of the cookie mixture on the baking sheet. Using a damp finger, press one of the reserved whole brazil nuts into the middle of each cookie. Bake for 10-12 minutes. Allow to cool a little before transferring to a baking rack – they crisp as they cool.

TIP

The basic ingredients make the difference: choose a high-quality cocoa powder and crack the nuts yourself.

Nutritional value per serving:

Calories: 158

Fats: 11g

Carbohydrates: 13g

Salt: 0.24g

index

acknowledgments

The publishers would like to thank the following authors for permission to use the recipes reproduced on the pages indicated: **Darina Allen:** 26, 98, 102, 114, 118, 142, 144, 154, 166; **Hugo Arnold:** 22, 24, 80, 82, 146; **Ed Baines:** 30, 56, 86, 148; **Vatcharin Bhumichitr:** 60, 72, 160; **Maddalena Bonino:** 40, 58; **Conrad Gallagher:** 14, 32, 38, 70, 128, 130, 132, 140; **Paul Gayler:** 16, 20, 36, 52, 62, 64, 76, 88, 90, 94, 96, 100, 104, 106, 110, 112, 134, 136, 158; **Elisabeth Luard:** 18, 68, 116, 162, 164, 168, 170; **Alison Price:** 42, 50, 54, 124, 138, 150; **Oded Schwartz:** 74, 156; **Mandy Wagstaff:** 34, 44, 46, 48, 78, 108, 120, 122; **Sarah Woodward:** 28, 84.

The publishers would like to thank the following photographers for permission to use the images reproduced on the pages indicated: **Martin Brigdale:** 7, 9, 61, 73, 161; **Julie Dixon:** 75, 157; **Gus Filgate:** 15, 29, 31, 33, 39, 53, 57, 63, 65, 71, 85, 87, 89, 91, 107, 129, 131, 133, 141, 149; **Michelle Garrett:** 41, 59; **Georgia Glynn-Smith:** 1, 17, 21, 37, 66, 77, 95, 97, 101, 111, 113, 126, 135, 137, 152, 159; **Jeremy Hopley:** 43, 51, 55, 125, 139, 151; **Francine Lawrence:** 19, 69, 117, 163, 165, 169, 171; **Ray Main:** 2, 5, 12, 23, 25, 27, 81, 83, 84, 92, 99, 103, 115, 119, 143, 145, 147, 154, 155, 166; **Jean-Luc Scotto:** 70, 72, 74, 78, 82, 84, 86, 92, 96, 106; **Sara Taylor:** 35, 45, 47, 49, 79, 109, 121, 123